The Marginal Spouse Series Book 3 " Becoming Whole Again"

Healing and Responsibility for the Marginal Spouse

Cynthia Davis Jones

Professional and Ministry Disclaimer

The content of this book reflects the author's biblical convictions, pastoral experience, and counseling insight. It is intended for spiritual formation, personal reflection, and educational purposes only.

This book does not constitute therapy, clinical diagnosis, medical treatment, legal counsel, or professional advice of any kind. Reading this material does not establish a counselor-client, therapist-client, pastoral care, or fiduciary relationship with the author.

If you are experiencing a mental health crisis, suicidal ideation, abuse, or medical emergency, seek immediate help by contacting emergency services or a licensed professional in your area.

Readers are responsible for how they apply the information presented. The author and publisher assume no responsibility for the misuse or misapplication of the material.

All identifiable personal details in illustrative stories have been changed to protect confidentiality.

Published by Life Change Press | USA

Scripture quotations are from the NASB unless otherwise noted.

ISBN: To be assigned

Printed in the United States of America.

Contents

The Marginal Spouse Series 5
Acknowledgments 7
Introduction 9
PASTORAL NOTE 13

Part One
AWAKENING TO RESPONSIBILITY

1. When Awareness Begins 49
2. From Awareness to Ownership 57
3. Listening Without Defending 63

Part Two
FACING THE DAMAGE

4. Accepting Consequences Without Resentment 71
5. Consistency Over Time 76
6. Learning to Repair Without Defensiveness 81

Part Three
REBUILDING TRUST AND SAFETY

7. Understanding Trust as a Process 89
8. Accountability That Leads to Growth 94
9. Rebuilding Safety Through Transparency 99

Part Four
IDENTITY AND INTERNAL TRANSFORMATION

10. Rebuilding Identity Beyond Old Patterns 107
11. Responding to Setbacks Without Returning to Old Patterns 111
12. Replacing Old Coping Strategies with Healthy Responses 116

Part Five
LIVING WHOLE AND SUSTAINING CHANGE
13. Learning to Lead with Humility 123
14. Rebuilding Emotional Availability 127
15. Repairing Trust Through Daily Faithfulness 131

Part Six
WALKING FORWARD IN WHOLENESS
16. Living Changed Without Managing Outcomes 137
17. When Change Is Tested Over Time 141
18. Walking in Integrity Regardless of Response 145

CONCLUSION 149
A CALL TO RENEWAL 151
GUIDED PRAYER 153
PRAYERS APPENDIX 165
Becoming Whole in Practice Worksheets 175
SCRIPTURE INDEX 185
WEEKLY SCRIPTURE MEMORY PLAN 193
A WORD OF ENCOURAGEMENT 203
Continue the Journey Series Closing 205
BIBLIOGRAPHY 207
Suggested Reading: 209

The Marginal Spouse Series

Book One - The Marginal Spouse: Restoring Hope and Responsibility in Christian Marriage

Book Two - Living with a Marginal Spouse: Biblical Wisdom, Boundaries, and Hope for the Spouse Who Feels Alone

Book Three - Becoming Whole Again: Healing and Responsibility for the Marginal Spouse

Acknowledgments

BECOMING WHOLE AGAIN

Healing and Responsibility for the Marginal Spouse

This book is dedicated to those who have chosen honesty over avoidance and responsibility over defensiveness. Acknowledging the need for change is not easy, and choosing to pursue wholeness requires courage. I honor every reader who is willing to examine their patterns and submit them to God's transforming work.

I am thankful for the counselors, teachers, and faithful believers who have demonstrated that grace and accountability are not opposites. Your steady commitment to truth has reinforced the belief that genuine repentance leads to maturity, not shame.

Above all, I give thanks to God, who does not abandon the work He begins. This book reflects His patience, His faithfulness, and His ability to restore those who are willing to walk honestly before Him.

Introduction

BECOMING WHOLE AGAIN

Change rarely begins with confidence.

It often begins with discomfort.

If you are reading this book, something has likely shifted within you. Perhaps the patterns you once explained now feel heavier. Possibly, the reactions that once felt justified no longer bring peace. Or maybe you have been confronted by a spouse, by consequences, or by the quiet conviction of God, and you are beginning to recognize that the issue is not only the marriage.

It is you.

That realization can be unsettling. Shame may surface. Defensiveness may rise. The urge to explain, justify, or redirect responsibility can feel immediate and familiar. Yet your presence here suggests something important. Awareness has begun, and with it comes an invitation.

This book is not written to condemn you.

It is written to call you to the truth.

Marginal behavior in marriage is rarely the result of a single failure. It is most often a pattern of response. These patterns may include emotional withdrawal, silence, avoidance of responsibility, blame shifting, inconsistency, or control. Over time, these ways of relating erode trust, damage intimacy, and leave confusion and pain in their wake. They also fracture the inner life of the one who lives within them.

Scripture reminds us that transformation begins within.

> *"Create in me a clean heart, O God, and renew a steadfast spirit within me."*

Psalm 51:10 NASB

Becoming whole again requires more than good intentions. It requires ownership. Healing does not begin when others respond differently or when circumstances improve. It begins when you stop managing appearances and start facing reality with humility before God.

True wholeness is not about perfection. It is about integrity. It is about living honestly before the Lord and others, even when that honesty is uncomfortable.

> *"The one who conceals his wrongdoings will not prosper, but the one who confesses and abandons them will find compassion."*

Proverbs 28:13 NASB

This book will ask you to scrutinize your patterns. It will invite you to listen without defending, to accept responsibility without excuses, and to remain present rather than retreating when things feel exposed. It will also offer hope. Not the shallow hope of quick change, but the steady hope of transformation that unfolds over time through repentance, accountability, and obedience.

God is not interested in reshaping your image.

He is committed to restoring your heart.

> *"If anyone is in Christ, this person is a new creation. The old things passed away; behold, new things have come."*

2 Corinthians 5:17 NASB

Wholeness does not mean erasing the past. It means allowing God to redeem it. It means becoming a person whose character is no longer shaped by avoidance, control, or fear, but by truth, humility, and responsibility.

If you are willing to stay present, to resist the pull toward justification or withdrawal, and to submit honestly to God's work, this book will guide you toward becoming whole again, not simply for the sake of repairing a marriage, but for the sake of becoming a person who can love with integrity, consistency, and faithfulness.

Wholeness begins here.

PASTORAL NOTE

Before You Begin

This book asks you to do something difficult. It asks you to remain present to the truth rather than manage perception. It asks you to listen without preparing a defense. It asks you to consider responsibility not as punishment, but as a pathway to freedom.

If at any point you feel exposed, uncomfortable, or tempted to disengage, pause and bring that response before God. Those reactions are not obstacles to healing. They are often the very places where God is working.

> *"Search me, O God, and know my heart; put me to the test and know my anxious thoughts; and see if there is any harmful way in me and lead me in the everlasting way."*
>
> **Psalm 139:23–24 NASB**

You are not being asked to fix everything at once. You are being invited to walk honestly. Growth happens one step at a time, in humility, truth, and obedience.

Read slowly. Reflect honestly. Stay present.

THE SUFFICIENCY OF THE WORD OF GOD

There are seasons in marriage when human wisdom feels too small, too fragile, or too conflicted to guide you. People may misunderstand your pain, minimize your struggles, or offer advice that does not fit the reality of your marriage. But there is one source of truth that never bends under pressure, never changes with culture, and never misleads the weary heart:

The Word of God.

Scripture stands firm when emotions shift.

Scripture brings clarity when confusion rises.

Scripture provides wisdom when human voices contradict one another.

Scripture anchors your heart when relationships feel unstable.

Scripture reveals God's character when circumstances feel overwhelming.

The Word of God is not a last resort.

The Word of God is your foundation.

> *"All Scripture is inspired by God and beneficial for teaching, for rebuke, for correction, for training in righteousness."*

2 Timothy 3:16 NASB

The Word of God is sufficient because:

It reveals the truth

Truth exposes deception, confusion, and emotional manipulation.

It brings wisdom

God's Word guides your decisions when the path is unclear.

It strengthens your heart

Scripture restores hope when disappointment becomes heavy.

It protects your spirit

Biblical truth sets healthy, godly boundaries around your heart.

It aligns your emotions with God's perspective.

You learn to see your situation through His eyes, not your fear or exhaustion.

It reveals God's heart toward you.

Every page testifies to His compassion, His nearness, and His faithfulness.

In a marginal marriage, where communication wavers and relational clarity is unpredictable, God's Word remains steady.

It is the one voice you can trust, the one truth you can lean on, and the one foundation that cannot be shaken.

"Your word is a lamp to my feet and a light to my path."

Psalm 119:105 NASB

The path ahead may feel uncertain, but the lamp is steady.

God's Word will lead you, strengthen you, and sustain you one step at a time.

This portion has been adapted from Rich Thompson's *The Heart of Man and Mental Disorders.*

THE POINT OF CHOICE: PLEASING GOD OR PLEASING SELF

Every believer lives at a crossroads thousands of times a day in thoughts, words, responses, decisions, and desires. Scripture calls this crossroads **the point of choice**.

In every moment, whether in conflict or quiet, frustration or peace, you are choosing one of two paths:

The path of pleasing God

or

The path of pleasing the self

This is the heart of discipleship and of relational transformation.

"We make it our ambition... to be pleasing to Him."

2 Corinthians 5:9 NASB

Understanding this spiritual reality clarifies the dynamics of both the marginal spouse and the responsible spouse.

WHAT "PLEASING SELF" LOOKS LIKE IN THE MARGINAL SPOUSE

A marginal spouse often chooses a self-serving path without realizing it. This path is marked by:

- avoiding responsibility
- protecting comfort rather than protecting the relationship
- withdrawing instead of engaging
- defending instead of listening
- blaming instead of owning
- seeking relief instead of repentance
- serving emotion rather than truth

Pleasing oneself often feels easier in the moment, but it damages the marriage over time.

It prioritizes:

"My peace"
"My comfort"
"My image"
"My avoidance"
"My desires"

...overgrowth, connection, or biblical obedience.

This is why change can be so tricky for a marginal spouse:

Choosing to please God requires humility, surrender, and responsibility, all of which directly confront the inner life they've been avoiding.

What "Pleasing God" Would Look Like for the Marginal Spouse

If a marginal spouse chooses the path of pleasing God, signs might include:

- humility instead of defensiveness
- listening instead of denying
- taking responsibility instead of shifting blame
- repentance instead of excuses
- emotional engagement instead of withdrawal
- asking for help instead of hiding
- pursuing truth instead of comfort

Pleasing God requires courage to face what is broken and faith to trust God with the outcome.

This is repentance in motion.

What "Pleasing Self" Looks Like in the Responsible Spouse

The responsible spouse may not struggle with avoidance, but self-pleasing can still appear subtly in ways such as:

- over-functioning to avoid conflict
- sacrificing beyond biblical boundaries to maintain peace
- tolerating disrespect to prevent emotional eruption
- rescuing the marginal spouse to reduce personal anxiety
- trying to fix everything to feel secure
- equating self-worth with being needed
- collapsing inward out of exhaustion instead of seeking help

Self-pleasing isn't always selfish.

Sometimes it looks like **self-protection**,

self-salvation, or

Self-reliance.

In these moments, the responsible spouse may be trying to survive rather than trust God.

What "Pleasing God" Looks Like for the Responsible Spouse

For the responsible spouse, pleasing God includes:

- setting boundaries led by wisdom, not fear
- refusing to carry what belongs to their spouse
- speaking truth in love, not silence in exhaustion
- trusting God with the outcomes
- not rescuing or enabling
- honoring their own God-given worth
- choosing obedience over appeasement
- seeking support rather than suffering in isolation

Pleasing God produces strength, clarity, and peace, not burnout, resentment, or emotional collapse.

The Point of Choice Is Where Transformation Begins

Every moment in the marriage becomes a spiritual intersection:

Will I please God here?

Or will I please myself?

This applies when:

- A conflict begins
- A conversation shuts down
- Emotions rise
- Boundaries are tested
- Truth surfaces
- Responsibility is avoided
- Repentance is needed
- Hurt is expressed
- Exhaustion sets in

Pleasing God is not an emotional feeling.

It is a direction of the will. It changes everything.

God Meets You at the Point of Choice

You do not make these choices alone.

When you choose to please God:

- He strengthens you
- He comforts you
- He guides you
- He gives clarity
- He protects your heart
- He honors your obedience
- He works in the unseen places you cannot control

> *"It is God who is at work in you, both to will and to work for His good pleasure."*

Philippians 2:13 NASB

God empowers what He commands.

Every moment is a Point of Choice: to please God or to please self. The marginal spouse chooses self when avoiding responsibility; the responsible spouse chooses self when rescuing beyond wisdom. But when either spouse decides to please God, truth emerges, boundaries strengthen, repentance deepens, and healing becomes possible.

Portions of this section have been adapted from Dr. Nicolas Ellen's *Common Issues We Face*

PRIDE AND HUMILITY

Assessing the Heart After the Point of Choice

The point of choice marks a turning.

It is the moment when awareness gives way to decision. It is where the marginal spouse no longer asks whether change is necessary, but whether it will be pursued with honesty and endurance. From this point forward, the journey toward wholeness is no longer theoretical. It becomes lived.

What determines whether that journey leads to transformation or stagnation is not effort alone. It is a heart-posture.

From this point on, pride and humility will serve as ongoing indicators of direction. They will reveal whether growth is approached as surrender or self-management, as obedience or performance.

Scripture makes this distinction clear.

> *"God is opposed to the proud but gives grace to the humble."*

James 4:6 NASB

After the point of choice, pride often resurfaces quietly. It may sound reasonable or restrained. It may appear as impatience with consequences, frustration with slow progress, or fatigue with accountability. Pride may insist that effort should now produce relief, that acknowledgment should restore access, or that consistency should be rewarded. These responses do not signal failure; they indicate where the heart requires further examination.

Humility responds differently.

Humility accepts that the journey toward wholeness unfolds over time. It remains teachable when correction is repeated. It stays accountable when progress feels unseen. It allows trust to rebuild without pressure. Humility does not measure obedience by outcome. It measures it by faithfulness.

> *"Humble yourselves in the presence of the Lord, and He will exalt you."*

James 4:10 NASB

As you progress through this book, pride and humility should be assessed regularly. They will appear in how you listen, how you accept responsibility, how you respond to limits, and how you endure seasons where trust is still forming. Pride seeks control. Humility releases it. Pride explains. Humility owns. Pride manages appearances. Humility submits to truth.

This assessment is not meant to produce shame. It is intended to provide clarity. Pride resists exposure because it confuses accountability with condemnation. Humility understands that exposure is often the very place where healing deepens.

> *"Search me, O God, and know my heart; try me and know my anxious thoughts; and see if there be any hurtful way in me and lead me in the everlasting way."*
>
> **Psalm 139:23–24 NASB**

The pages that follow are designed to help you pause and reflect on your heart posture as you move forward. They will ask you to notice where pride still influences responses and where humility must be practiced intentionally. This work is not a detour from restoration. It is part of it.

Restoration does not advance through control.

Transformation does not endure through performance.

Wholeness grows where humility is chosen again and again after the point of choice.

As you engage in this book, remain honest, slow, and prayerful. Let humility guide the journey ahead.

IDOLS OF THE HEART

When Desire Replaces Devotion and Marriage Begins to Fracture

Marital breakdown rarely begins with one dramatic event. More often, it begins quietly in the heart. When desires slowly replace devotion to God, the heart begins to look elsewhere for meaning, relief, or fulfillment. Scripture identifies these misplaced desires as idols.

Idols of the heart are not always visible. They are not limited to objects or behaviors. They are the internal attachments we depend on more than we do on God. They are the things we believe must change, be restored, or be preserved for us to feel whole, safe, or satisfied.

"You shall have no other gods before Me."

Exodus 20:3 NASB

This command addresses more than worship practices. It speaks to allegiance. Whenever something takes the place of God as our source of security, identity, or hope, it becomes an idol.

HOW IDOLS FORM IN THE HEART

Idols often begin as legitimate desires. Desire itself is not sinful. God created us with longings for love, connection, peace, and purpose. The problem arises when a desire becomes a demand, leading us to believe we cannot be content or faithful unless that desire is fulfilled in a particular way.

In marriage, common heart idols include:

- The desire to be understood or validated
- The desire for emotional safety or control
- The desire for affection, intimacy, or approval
- The desire for peace without conflict
- The desire for restoration on our terms

When these desires eclipse trust in God, the heart subtly shifts. Instead of seeking God's will, we begin to protect our desires. When those desires are threatened or unmet, emotional distress follows.

FROM IDOLATRY TO HOPELESSNESS

When a heart idol is threatened, disappointment deepens into hopelessness. The person begins to believe that if this desire remains unfulfilled, life cannot be good, meaningful, or whole.

Hope shifts away from God and onto the desired outcome.

> *"Cursed is the man who trusts in mankind and makes flesh his strength, And whose heart turns away from the Lord."*
>
> **Jeremiah 17:5 NASB**

In marriage, this often appears when one spouse believes peace, happiness, or identity depends entirely on the other's behavior. When change does not occur as hoped, discouragement takes root. Hope diminishes, and despair begins to settle in.

FROM IDOLATRY TO ANGER

Unmet idols do not remain passive. They produce anger.

Anger arises when the heart believes it is being denied something it deserves or requires. When desires become demands, unmet expectations feel like injustice. The spouse, rather than the idol, becomes the perceived obstacle.

James explains this progression clearly.

> *"What is the source of quarrels and conflicts among you? Is not the source your pleasures that wage war in your members?"*

James 4:1 NASB

Anger fueled by idolatry often expresses itself through criticism, withdrawal, control, or bitterness. The issue may appear relational, but the root is spiritual. The heart is no longer submitting to the desire of God. It is demanding fulfillment from another person.

FROM IDOLATRY TO DESPAIR

When anger does not produce change, despair often follows. The heart grows weary of hoping and begins to harden. This is where emotional withdrawal, resignation, and relational distance deepen.

Scripture warns of this progression.

> *"Hope deferred makes the heart sick."*

Proverbs 13:12 NASB

Despair chips away at marriage quietly. Conversations grow shorter. Emotional availability fades. Faithfulness becomes mechanical. Without recognizing the role of heart idolatry, couples may misdiagnose the problem as incompatibility rather than misplaced devotion.

~

IDOLS AND THE MARGINAL SPOUSE

For the marginal spouse, heart idols often fuel avoidance, control, or withdrawal. The desire for comfort, autonomy, or peace without engagement becomes more important than obedience, humility, or presence. When God's call conflicts with personal desire, the idol quietly wins.

Yet Scripture consistently calls the heart back to proper alignment.

> *"Trust in the Lord with all your heart.*
> *And do not lean on your own understanding."*
>
> **Proverbs 3:5 NASB**

Trust requires surrender. It requires releasing control over outcomes and submitting desires to God's wisdom rather than insisting on fulfillment.

~

TURNING FROM IDOLS TO GOD

Repentance involves more than confessing behavior. It includes identifying and renouncing heart idols. This requires asking difficult questions.

What do I believe must change for me to be at peace?

What outcome am I demanding rather than trusting God with

What desire am I protecting even when it conflicts with obedience

Scripture invites this examination.

> *"Search me, O God, and know my heart;*
> *Try me and know my anxious thoughts."*

Psalm 139:23 NASB

As idols are exposed and surrendered, freedom begins. Hope is restored—not because circumstances change, but because trust is re-anchored in God.

~

RESTORATION BEGINS WITH REALIGNED DESIRE

God does not shame us for having desires. He invites us to submit them. When desires are rightly ordered under God, relationships are freed from the burden of meeting needs they were never designed to fulfill.

> "You will keep him in perfect peace,
> Whose mind is stayed on You,
> Because he trusts in You."

Isaiah 26:3 NASB

When God is restored to His rightful place, marriage becomes a context for growth rather than a source of identity. Anger softens. Hope revives. Despair loosens its grip.

Wholeness does not come from fulfilled idols.

It comes from surrendered hearts.

When idols of the heart are exposed, the next question is not whether we have desired wrongly, but how we respond when those desires are challenged. This is where pride and humility reveal themselves. Pride protects idols. It explains them, justifies them, and resists their removal. Humility surrenders them. It allows God to reorder the heart, even when letting go feels costly or uncertain.

The struggle with heart idolatry is not merely what we want. It is about who we trust. When desire becomes demand, pride quietly takes hold, insisting that peace, safety, or fulfillment must come on our terms. Humility responds differently. It acknowledges the disordered desire, releases control, and submits to God's wisdom rather than personal preference.

As you move into the next section, you are invited to examine not only what you desire, but how you hold those desires. Pride clings tightly and resists change. Humility opens the hands and invites God to reshape the heart. Restoration deepens where humility replaces self-protection and where surrendered desires make room for grace.

This transition marks a critical moment in the journey toward wholeness. The willingness to relinquish idols prepares the heart to receive the work of humility that follows.

WHAT I CAN AND CANNOT CONTROL

Responsibility, Surrender, and the Work of Becoming Whole

One of the greatest obstacles to healing for the marginal spouse is confusion about who is responsible. When responsibility is unclear, control quietly replaces obedience, and frustration replaces faithfulness. Learning what can and cannot be controlled is essential to becoming whole again.

God never calls His people to control outcomes.

He calls them to walk in obedience.

Understanding this distinction brings freedom. It removes the burden of managing others and places responsibility where it belongs, on the heart, choices, and conduct of the individual before God.

WHAT THE MARGINAL SPOUSE CANNOT CONTROL

The marginal spouse cannot control another person's heart, healing, or response. No amount of effort, explanation, consistency, or remorse can force trust to return or pain to resolve on a timeline.

The marginal spouse cannot control:

- Whether a spouse forgives quickly or slowly
- Whether trust is restored immediately or gradually
- How another person processes pain
- Whether reconciliation unfolds as hoped
- Whether past damage still affects present emotions
- How long healing takes

Attempting to control these outcomes often leads to frustration, resentment, or despair. Control may appear as pressure, withdrawal, emotional shutdown, or subtle manipulation. While these behaviors may feel protective, they undermine integrity and stall growth.

Scripture reminds us:

> "The heart of man plans his way,
> But the Lord directs his steps."

Proverbs 16:9 NASB

When the marginal spouse tries to manage results, faithfulness is replaced by performance. Obedience becomes conditional, and humility gives way to entitlement.

WHAT THE MARGINAL SPOUSE IS RESPONSIBLE FOR

While outcomes cannot be controlled, responsibility remains clear. God holds each person accountable not for results, but for faithfulness.

The marginal spouse **is responsible for**:

- Owning personal sin without explanation or comparison
- Repenting honestly before God
- Aligning behavior with truth, not emotion
- Practicing consistency rather than intensity
- Listening without defending
- Remaining emotionally present
- Accepting consequences without resentment
- Maintaining humility when trust is slow to rebuild
- Living with integrity regardless of response

Responsibility is not about proving change.

It is about living truthfully before God.

Scripture speaks plainly:

> *"So, then each one of us will give an account of himself to God."*

Romans 14:12 NASB

Responsibility does not end when discomfort appears. It is sustained through obedience, patience, and surrender.

~

CONTROL VERSUS INTEGRITY

Control asks, *What must happen for me to feel at peace*

Integrity asks, *What does obedience require of me right now*

Control focuses on outcomes.

Integrity focuses on alignment.

When the marginal spouse shifts from control to integrity, internal pressure begins to lift. Growth becomes steadier. Faithfulness becomes quieter. The heart learns to rest in obedience rather than results.

> *"Commit your works to the Lord*
> *And your plans will be established."*

Proverbs 16:3 NASB

This does not mean the marginal spouse disengages or becomes passive. It means engagement is no longer driven by fear, entitlement, or urgency. It is shaped by wisdom and submission to God.

~

ACCEPTING RESPONSIBILITY WITHOUT MANAGING RESULTS

A critical step toward wholeness is accepting that responsibility and control are not the same.

Responsibility says:

I will do what God calls me to do, even when it is difficult.

Control says:

I will do whatever it takes to get the response I want.

Only one of these produces lasting change.

Jesus Himself modeled this posture:

"Not My will, but Yours be done."

Luke 22:42 NASB

True growth requires surrender. When the marginal spouse relinquishes control and assumes responsibility, humility deepens, and integrity strengthens. Trust is no longer demanded. It is allowed to rebuild naturally over time.

~

LIVING WITH CLARITY AND FREEDOM

Knowing what you can and cannot control brings peace. It clarifies expectations and removes the hidden pressure to manage outcomes. It allows the marginal spouse to focus on what God has entrusted to them: their heart, choices, and obedience.

Wholeness does not come from fixing everything.

It comes from being faithful in what is yours to carry.

OPEN AND CLOSED LOVING

How Our Posture Toward God Shapes Every Relationship

Every person lives from a posture of the heart. First and foremost, the confession of sin to God and the control of the Holy Spirit, who produces God's love in man's heart. As we sin daily, we should confess accordingly. As we develop this life pattern of walking in love, we will experience peace, confidence, and a desire to draw near to God. Expressions of love develop our character and expose what's in our hearts. We should choose to express openly the love which God produces in our hearts for each other.

Before love can be open or closed in marriage, it is already open or closed toward God. The way a person responds to God's truth, correction, grace, and presence determines how they will react to a spouse, to accountability, and to intimacy. Loving does not originate in marriage. It flows from the heart's posture toward God. In other words, man should have an open and loving relationship with God.

Scripture makes this order clear.

"We love, because He first loved us."

1 John 4:19 NASB

When the marginal spouse struggles to love openly in marriage, the issue is rarely limited to relational skills. More often, it reflects a deeper posture toward God. A heart that remains guarded, defensive, or selective before God will carry that same posture into human relationships.

~

AN OPEN AND LOVING POSTURE TOWARD GOD

The Source of Wholeness

An open and loving relationship with God is marked by humility, surrender, and trust. It does not require perfection, but it does require honesty.

This posture looks like:

- Welcoming God's examination rather than resisting it
- Receiving correction without defensiveness
- Confessing sin without minimizing it
- Trusting God with outcomes rather than controlling them

David modeled this posture when he prayed,

> *"Search me, O God, and know my heart; try me and know my anxious thoughts."*

Psalm 139:23 NASB

When the heart is open and loving toward God, grace flows freely. God can convict, restore, and transform without resistance.

> *"God is opposed to the proud but gives grace to the humble."*

James 4:6 NASB

This grace does not stop with the individual. It shapes how the marginal spouse listens, repents, remains accountable, and loves others. An open and loving posture toward God fosters humility that naturally manifests in relationships.

~

A CLOSED POSTURE TOWARD GOD

Where Loving Begins to Fracture

A closed posture toward God often develops quietly. It may coexist with religious language, church attendance, or moral effort. Yet the heart remains guarded.

This posture may include:

- Avoiding conviction
- Explaining rather than repenting
- Selective obedience
- Resistance to correction
- Managing image rather than submitting to truth

When the heart closes toward God, it does not remain open toward people. The same defensiveness that resists God's truth resists a spouse's pain. The same avoidance that limits repentance before God limits vulnerability in marriage.

Scripture warns of this danger.

> *"Today if you hear His voice, do not harden your hearts."*

Hebrews 3:15 NASB

A hardened heart toward God will eventually harden toward others.

~

HOW POSTURE TOWARD GOD SHAPES LOVING IN MARRIAGE

Once a posture toward God is established, it flows outward. The four relational postures seen in marriage are rooted in how the heart engages God.

~

OPEN AND LOVING WITH GOD

OPEN AND LOVING WITH OTHERS

When a person remains open and loving toward God, love naturally flows outward.

In marriage, this posture looks like:

- Listening without defending
- Owning impact without excuse
- Remaining emotionally present
- Accepting accountability with humility
- Staying faithful without controlling outcomes

This posture reflects God's design.

> *"You shall love the Lord your God with all your heart... and your neighbor as yourself."*
>
> **Matthew 22:37–39 NASB**

Love toward God fuels love toward others.

~

CLOSED WITH GOD

CLOSED BUT CLAIMING TO LOVE OTHERS

A person may believe they love their spouse while remaining closed toward God. This results in closed and loving behavior that lacks depth.

In marriage, this posture often looks like:

- Providing without emotional availability
- Politeness without intimacy
- Stability without vulnerability
- Care without engagement

This posture limits healing because love remains controlled rather than surrendered.

OPEN WITH GOD

OPEN BUT UNLOVING WITH OTHERS

In some cases, a person may be emotionally expressive or verbally honest, yet unloving in tone and impact. This often reflects partial openness toward God that lacks submission.

Truth is spoken, but humility is missing.

Scripture corrects this imbalance.

> *"Speaking the truth in love, we are to grow up in all aspects into Him."*

Ephesians 4:15 NASB

Openness without love wounds rather than heals. To correct this unloving attitude and behavior, confession and repentance before God are required.

CLOSED WITH GOD

CLOSED AND UNLOVING WITH OTHERS

When the heart remains closed toward God over time, love toward others often diminishes. Resentment, withdrawal, and indifference take root.

This posture reflects spiritual resistance, not merely relational fatigue.

> *"Whoever hates his brother is in the darkness and walks in the darkness."*
>
> **1 John 2:11 NASB**

Without confession and repentance, this posture erodes connection and blocks restoration.

THE CALL TO REALIGN

Becoming whole again requires realignment, not only in marriage but first before God.

Restoration does not begin by trying harder to love a spouse.

It begins by opening the heart fully to God.

As the marginal spouse learns to live openly and lovingly before God, humility increases, defensiveness decreases, and love becomes less controlled and more sincere. What God transforms vertically will inevitably reshape what is expressed horizontally.

"Above all, keep fervent in your love for one another."

1 Peter 4:8 NASB

This love is not self-generated.

It is God-formed.

TRUE REPENTANCE BEFORE GOD

The Pathway to Genuine Transformation

Repentance is not a moment of regret.

It is a turning of the heart that results in a changed direction.

In Scripture, repentance is never presented as mere remorse, emotional sorrow, or verbal apology. True repentance is a spiritual act that begins before God and reshapes how a person lives, responds, and relates. Without repentance, awareness stagnates, responsibility wanes, and change is temporary. With repentance, transformation becomes possible.

The marginal spouse must clearly understand this. Restoration in marriage does not begin with promises, explanations, or improved behavior alone. It starts with true repentance before God.

REPENTANCE BEGINS WITH GOD, NOT WITH RELIEF

True repentance is first vertical, not horizontal. It is a response to God's holiness rather than a reaction to consequences. When repentance is motivated primarily by discomfort, loss, or pressure, it often fades once relief appears. Biblical repentance is motivated by truth.

David modeled this posture when he said,

> *"Against You, You only, I have sinned*
> *And done what is evil in Your sight."*

Psalms 51:4 NASB

David did not deny the harm done to others. He placed responsibility where it belonged first, before God. True repentance acknowledges that sin is ultimately a violation of God's truth and character.

Repentance that begins before God does not ask, *How do I feel about this*

It asks, *what does God say is true.*

GODLY SORROW VERSUS WORLDLY SORROW

Scripture distinguishes clearly between sorrow that transforms and sorrow that merely reacts.

> *"For the sorrow that is according to the will of God produces a repentance without regret, leading to salvation, but the sorrow of the world produces death."*

2 Corinthians 7:10 NASB

Worldly sorrow focuses on loss, embarrassment, or consequences. It often says, *I regret what happened.* Godly sorrow focuses on truth and affirms, "I see my sin as God sees it." One seeks relief. The other seeks alignment.

The marginal spouse may feel genuine sadness about the harm caused, yet still resist repentance if defensiveness, justification, or entitlement persist. Godly sorrow removes excuses. It does not negotiate responsibility.

REPENTANCE INVOLVES CONFESSION WITHOUT DEFENSE

True repentance includes an honest and complete confession. Confession does not explain. It does not compare. It does not minimize.

> *"He who conceals his transgressions will not prosper,*
> *But he who confesses and forsakes them will find*
> *compassion."*
>
> **Proverbs 28:13 NASB**

Confession before God names sin clearly and takes responsibility for its impact. It does not focus on intent. It focuses on truth. Where confession is partial, repentance remains incomplete.

For the marginal spouse, confession may feel threatening because it removes a sense of self-protection. Yet Scripture consistently shows that confession is the doorway to mercy, not condemnation.

REPENTANCE REQUIRES TURNING, NOT JUST ADMITTING

The biblical term for repentance denotes a change of direction. It is not agreement with truth alone, but movement in response to it.

Peter preached repentance this way,

> *"Therefore, repent and return, so that your sins may be wiped away."*

Acts 3:19 NASB

True repentance results in observable change. Not perfection, but direction. Not intensity, but consistency. Where behavior remains unchanged, repentance has not yet taken root.

This does not mean change happens instantly. It means the heart no longer protects the sin it confesses. Repentance removes permission for old patterns to remain.

REPENTANCE ACCEPTS CONSEQUENCES WITHOUT DEMAND

Biblical repentance does not negotiate outcomes. It does not demand restored trust, relief, or reassurance as proof of forgiveness. It accepts consequences as part of God's refining work.

When Zacchaeus repented, his repentance moved him to repair harm without being asked.

> *"If I have defrauded anyone of anything, I will give back four times as much."*

Luke 19:8 NASB

Repentance that resists consequence often reveals lingering pride. Repentance that accepts consequences demonstrates humility and sincerity.

REPENTANCE PRODUCES HUMILITY AND DEPENDENCE

True repentance leaves the heart tender rather than defensive. It produces humility rather than shame, and dependence rather than self-reliance.

> *"The sacrifices of God are a broken spirit;*
> *A broken and a contrite heart, O God, You will not*
> *despise."*

Psalms 51:17 NASB

A contrite heart remains teachable. It stays accountable. It welcomes correction. It does not rush the restoration process.

For the marginal spouse, this humility becomes the foundation for rebuilding trust, practicing open-heartedness, and living differently without managing outcomes.

REPENTANCE IS ONGOING, NOT ONE-TIME

Scripture does not present repentance as a single event. It is a posture maintained over time. Growth requires repeatedly returning to truth when pride, defensiveness, or avoidance resurface.

Jesus said,

> *"Repent, for the kingdom of heaven is at hand."*

Matthew 4:17 NASB

This call was not limited to unbelievers. It describes the continual posture of those who are called according to His purpose.

True repentance keeps the heart aligned even when change is tested.

TRUE REPENTANCE AND THE JOURNEY TO WHOLENESS

Becoming whole again is impossible without repentance that is honest, humble, and enduring. Repentance clears the ground for healing. It removes resistance. It creates space for God to work deeply rather than superficially.

Repentance does not earn forgiveness.

It receives it.

Repentance does not restore relationships instantly.

It makes restoration possible.

When repentance is genuine, transformation follows. Slowly. Faithfully. By God's grace.

Part One

AWAKENING TO RESPONSIBILITY

Chapter 1

When Awareness Begins

Change does not begin with repentance.

It begins with awareness.

Before responsibility is accepted, something must first be recognized. Patterns must be named. Reactions must be examined. The story we tell ourselves about our behavior must be brought into the light.

Awareness is often uncomfortable because it disrupts familiar explanations. It challenges long-held narratives. It calls into question the reasons we have used to justify distance, silence, control, or avoidance. Yet awareness is not condemnation. It is the first evidence that truth is breaking through.

> *"For the word of God is living and active, and sharper than any two-edged sword, and piercing as far as the division of soul and spirit, of both joints and marrow, and able to judge the thoughts and intentions of the heart."*

Hebrews 4:12 NASB

Marginal behavior rarely appears all at once. It develops over time through repeated choices. Choices to withdraw rather than engage. Choices to protect oneself rather than pursue understanding. Choices to manage conflict rather than address it. Over time, these choices form patterns, and patterns shape character.

Awareness begins when those patterns are no longer invisible.

You may begin to notice how often you deflect responsibility. How quickly do you explain your actions instead of listening? How silence has become a form of control rather than a source of peace. Or how inconsistency has replaced faithfulness. These realizations can feel threatening, particularly if you have relied on these patterns to feel safe or in control.

Scripture does not minimize the weight of self-examination.

> *"Examine yourselves to see whether you are in the faith; test yourselves."*

2 Corinthians 13:5 NASB

This examination is not meant to produce shame. It is intended to create clarity. Shame drives hiding. Clarity invites repentance. Until awareness takes place, change remains superficial and temporary.

Many marginal spouses believe change means improving behavior while preserving the same internal posture. That approach rarely leads to transformation. Actual change requires a willingness to see oneself accurately, without distortion, excuses, or comparison.

> *"When pride comes, then comes dishonor, but with the humble there is wisdom."*
>
> **Proverbs 11:2 NASB**

Awareness is an act of humility. It is the willingness to admit that your ways of responding, coping, or relating may have caused harm, even if that was not your intent. Intent does not erase impact. Love requires responsibility for both.

Becoming whole again begins when you stop asking how little you must change and start asking what truth requires.

This chapter is not about fixing your spouse, repairing the relationship, or restoring outcomes. It is about recognizing reality. Until reality is faced, healing cannot proceed.

Awareness is not the end of the journey.

It is the door.

Reflection

What patterns in your behavior are becoming harder to ignore?

Where do you feel most defensive as you read this chapter?

What explanations have you relied on to avoid responsibility?

What would it look like to ask God for clarity rather than comfort?

"Therefore, if anyone is in Christ, this person is a new creation; the old things passed away; behold, new things have come."

2 Corinthians 5:17 NASB

BIBLICAL INSIGHT

Truth That Reveals the Heart

Scripture consistently teaches that God's work of change begins internally before it ever becomes visible externally. Awareness is not a purely psychological concept. It is a spiritual one. God brings awareness not to condemn, but to invite repentance and restoration.

When Adam and Eve sinned, God's first response was not punishment. It was a question.

"Where are you?"

Genesis 3:9 NASB

That question was not for God's information. It was an invitation for Adam to become aware of his condition and to respond honestly. Awareness precedes responsibility.

Throughout Scripture, God calls His people to self-examination before He calls them to action.

"Let us examine and probe our ways, and let us return to the Lord,"

Lamentations 3:40 NASB

Awareness that leads nowhere produces guilt. Awareness that leads to God produces repentance. Repentance is not merely feeling regret. It is a turning of the heart that results in a changed direction.

True repentance begins when you stop comparing yourself to others and begin responding to God. It requires humility. It requires truth-telling. And it requires the courage to let God expose what you have long avoided.

Awareness is not weakness.

It is evidence that God is working.

COUNSELING INSIGHT

Acknowledging Responsibility Without Defensiveness

From a counseling perspective, the first and most critical step toward becoming whole again is acknowledging responsibility without defensiveness. Many marginal spouses initially recognize that something is wrong but remain guarded when responsibility is assigned. Defensiveness often takes the form of justification, minimization, comparison, or spiritual language that bypasses accountability.

True responsibility requires more than admitting mistakes. It requires ownership of impact. Counseling emphasizes that healing begins when an individual can not only say what they intended but also how their behavior affected others.

Defensiveness protects self-image but blocks growth. When a person remains focused on explaining themselves, they cannot hear others' pain.

Defensiveness protects self-image but blocks growth. When a person remains focused on explaining themselves, they cannot hear others' pain. Counseling helps individuals recognize that responsibility is distinct from condemnation. It is the foundation of change.

Another common observation in counseling is that marginal spouses often conflate remorse with repentance. Feeling regret does not automatically lead to transformation. Repentance involves a change in thinking, direction, and behavior over time.

This chapter marks the transition from awareness to accountability. Without this shift, progress will remain superficial.

COUNSELING APPLICATION

Moving from Insight to Ownership

1. Internal Awareness (Heart Work)
The marginal spouse begins by noticing internal reactions when discomfort becomes aware. This includes recognizing urges to explain, justify, withdraw, or minimize. Instead of responding immediately, the marginal spouse pauses to identify what emotion or belief is being protected.

2. Behavioral Shift (Observable Action)
The marginal spouse practices replacing explanations with acknowledgment. Rather than clarifying intent, the marginal spouse's name continues to affect and remain present without defense.

3. Relational Practice (How Others Experience Change)
The spouse experiences safety when the marginal spouse listens without correcting or redirecting. Presence without explanation signals sincerity.

4. Sustainability Check (Accountability and Consistency)
The marginal spouse commits to regular reflection and shares awareness patterns with a counselor or accountability partner.

GUIDED PRAYER

A Prayer for Awareness and Honesty

Take a moment to slow your breathing.

Allow yourself to be still before God.

Lord God,

I come to You with a heart that is beginning to see. I confess that awareness is uncomfortable for me. I have relied on explanations, defenses, and avoidance to protect myself. I ask You now to help me lay those down.

Search my heart and reveal what I have ignored or justified. Please give me the courage to see myself truthfully, without distortion or fear. Where I have withdrawn, show me why. Where I have controlled, please help me understand what I was protecting. Where I have caused harm, give me humility to acknowledge it.

Create in me a clean heart, O God, and renew a steadfast spirit within me. Teach me to listen without defending and to remain present when truth is complicated.

I ask not for relief, but for clarity.

Not for control, but for transformation.

Not for excuses, but for repentance that leads to life.

I place myself before You, trusting that You discipline those You love and restore those who are willing to walk in truth.

In Jesus' name,
Amen.

Chapter 2

From Awareness to Ownership

Awareness opens the door.

Ownership requires you to walk through it.

Many people acknowledge that something is wrong. Far fewer are willing to accept responsibility for their role in it. Awareness says, "I see the pattern." Ownership says, "This pattern belongs to me, and I am accountable for changing it."

Ownership is where defensiveness is tested. It is the moment when explanations must give way to responsibility. At this stage, many marginal spouses stall. They remain aware but avoid commitment. They agree that change is needed, but resist incurring personal costs. They want understanding without accountability.

Scripture does not separate awareness from ownership.

> *"So, then each one of us will give an account of himself to God."*

Romans 14:12 NASB

Ownership means you stop focusing on what others should do and begin addressing what God is calling you to do. It is not about assigning blame or accepting all fault indiscriminately. It is about responding honestly to your part, without comparison or excuse.

One of the clearest indicators of ownership is how you respond when confronted. Do you listen, or do you defend? Do you reflect, or do you redirect? Do you take responsibility, or do you minimize the impact of your behavior?

Ownership requires courage because it removes the safety net of self-justification. Yet it is also where freedom begins.

> *"The one who conceals his wrongdoings will not prosper, but the one who confesses and abandons them will find compassion."*

Proverbs 28:13, NASB

Becoming whole again means learning to stand in truth without collapsing into shame or rising into pride. Ownership is not self-punishment. It is in alignment with reality.

BIBLICAL INSIGHT

Responsibility Before God

Throughout Scripture, God calls His people to take responsibility for their actions without deflection. When Nathan confronted David, he did not explain his behavior or point to the circumstances. He responded truthfully.

"I have sinned against the Lord."

2 Samuel 12:13 NASB

That response did not erase consequences, but it opened the door to restoration. God responds to ownership with mercy, not indulgence.

Ownership acknowledges that sin and harmful patterns affect others. Scripture teaches that repentance involves confession and turning, not merely sorrow.

"For the sorrow that is according to the will of God produces a repentance without regret, leading to salvation."

2 Corinthians 7:10 NASB

Ownership before God produces humility. Humility produces teachability. Teachability allows change to take root.

COUNSELING INSIGHT

Why Change Feels Impossible

From a counseling perspective, many marginal spouses experience internal resistance when confronted with the need for change. This resistance is often misinterpreted as stubbornness or unwillingness, when in reality it is frequently rooted in fear, emotional immaturity, and long-standing coping patterns.

Change feels impossible when avoidance has been used as a protective measure. Marginal spouses often rely on emotional withdrawal, distraction, or minimization to regulate discomfort. These strategies may have once felt necessary, but over time, they become barriers to growth.

Counseling indicates that change becomes threatening when it requires confronting internal deficits, such as emotional awareness, empathy, or consistency. Rather than acknowledging these gaps, the marginal spouse may focus on external circumstances or relational dynamics to explain stagnation.

Another counseling observation is that marginal spouses often underestimate the cumulative impact of small behaviors. Because the harm was neither dramatic nor intentional, they may struggle to understand why change is necessary. Counseling reframes this by emphasizing that patterns, not isolated incidents, shape relationships.

This chapter helps the marginal spouse recognize that feeling stuck does not mean change is impossible. It often implies that change has not yet been approached honestly or intentionally.

COUNSELING APPLICATION

Practicing Responsibility Without Excuses

1. Internal Awareness (Heart Work)
The marginal spouse identifies resistance to ownership, especially thoughts that shift responsibility or expect quick relief.

2. Behavioral Shift (Observable Action)
The marginal spouse replaces vague admissions with specific acknowledgment of behaviors and patterns.

3. Relational Practice (How Others Experience Change)
Ownership is demonstrated by accepting limited trust without pressure or resentment.

4. Sustainability Check (Accountability and Consistency)
The marginal spouse invites ongoing accountability focused on consistency rather than explanation.

GUIDED PRAYER

A Prayer for Responsibility

Lord God,

I acknowledge that awareness alone is not enough. I ask you for the courage to move from seeing to owning. Please help me stop explaining my behavior and begin taking responsibility for it.

Where I have minimized harm, please show me the truth. Where I have defended myself, teach me humility. Where I have delayed change, please give me the conviction to act.

Teach me to accept responsibility without collapsing into shame or protecting myself with pride. Shape my heart so that ownership becomes a pathway to freedom rather than fear.

I place my actions, my patterns, and my choices before You. Lead me in repentance that results in lasting change.

In Jesus' name,
Amen.

Reflecting on Ownership

Use the space below to write honestly. Do not rush. Do not edit yourself.

- What behaviors or patterns do I need to take responsibility for
- Where have I offered explanations instead of ownership
- What fears arise when I consider full responsibility
- How might ownership change the way I respond to my spouse
- What would consistent responsibility look like in daily life

Chapter 3

Listening Without Defending

One of the clearest indicators of genuine change is the ability to listen without defending.

Defensiveness is a reflex. It rises quickly when we feel exposed, misunderstood, or threatened. For many marginal spouses, defensiveness has served as a protective mechanism. It has helped you maintain control, preserve self-image, or avoid discomfort. Over time, however, defensiveness becomes a barrier to truth and intimacy.

Listening without defending does not mean agreeing with everything that is said. It means resisting the urge to explain yourself while someone else is speaking. It means allowing another person's experience to exist without correction, comparison, or qualification.

Scripture consistently connects listening with wisdom.

> *"One who answers before he hears, it is foolishness and shame to him."*

Proverbs 18:13 NASB

When your spouse speaks about pain, disappointment, or fear, your instinct may be to respond with intent. You may want to clarify what you meant, what you were dealing with, or why their interpretation feels inaccurate. While intent matters, it does not erase impact. Listening without defending allows impact to be acknowledged without argument.

Defensiveness often sounds reasonable. It may appear calm, logical, or explanatory. Yet beneath it is usually fear. Fear of being wrong. Fear of being seen. Fear of losing power or position. Healing requires the courage to remain present with discomfort rather than escaping through explanation.

Listening is an act of humility. It communicates that the other person's experience matters, even when it is complicated to hear.

> *"Let everyone be quick to hear, slow to speak, and slow to anger."*

James 1:19, NASB

This kind of listening creates space. Space for truth. Space for repentance. Space for rebuilding trust. Trust does not grow when pain is debated. It grows when pain is honored.

Listening without defending does not guarantee reconciliation. It does, however, demonstrate maturity. It signals a shift from self-protection to responsibility.

Becoming whole again requires learning to hear without controlling the narrative.

BIBLICAL INSIGHT

Hearing Before Speaking

Throughout Scripture, God repeatedly calls His people to listen before responding. Listening is not passive. It is an act of submission and reverence.

When Job demanded explanations from God, God responded not with immediate answers but by redirecting Job toward humility and perspective. Job's transformation began when he stopped arguing and began listening.

> *"I have heard of You by the hearing of the ear; but now my eye sees You."*
>
> **Job 42:5 NASB**

Hearing precedes seeing, and listening precedes understanding.

Jesus Himself modeled listening. He asked questions. He allowed people to speak. He did not rush to defend His authority or correct every misunderstanding. He responded from truth rather than insecurity.

Listening without defending reflects trust in God's justice rather than reliance on self-protection. It demonstrates faith that truth does not require management.

COUNSELING INSIGHT

Why Defensiveness Blocks Healing

From a counseling perspective, defensiveness is one of the most significant barriers to relational repair. When a person defends, the other person feels dismissed. Their experience is challenged rather than received. Over time, this leads to emotional shutdown or escalation.

Defensiveness communicates, even unintentionally, that self-protection matters more than connection.

Many marginal spouses confuse listening with surrendering power. In reality, listening increases credibility. When you can hear brutal truths without reacting, you demonstrate emotional regulation and maturity.

Counseling work emphasizes this principle. You do not need to agree to listen. You need to be present. Presence communicates safety. Safety allows honesty. Honesty is necessary for trust.

Learning to listen without defending requires practice. It may feel unnatural at first. Silence may feel exposed. Yet silence can also be a powerful demonstration of respect.

COUNSELING APPLICATION

Developing Non-Defensive Listening

1. Internal Awareness (Heart Work)
The marginal spouse notices physical and emotional signs of defensiveness and chooses to be restrained.

2. Behavioral Shift (Observable Action)
The marginal spouse listens attentively before responding and refrains from interrupting or correcting.

3. Relational Practice (How Others Experience Change)
The spouse experiences validation through attentive silence and empathy.

4. Sustainability Check (Accountability and Consistency)
The marginal spouse reflects after conversations to evaluate presence rather than agreement.

GUIDED PRAYER

A Prayer for Humble Listening

Lord God,

I confess that listening is difficult for me when I feel criticized or exposed. I ask You to quiet my need to defend myself and help me remain present with truth.

Teach me to listen without interrupting, correcting, or explaining. Give me humility to receive another person's experience without comparison or dismissal. Help me trust that You are my defender, and that I do not need to protect myself from every uncomfortable truth.

Shape my heart to value understanding over control and connection over image. May my listening reflect Your patience and wisdom.

In Jesus' name,
Amen.

Reflecting on Listening

Take time to write honestly.

- When do I feel most defensive in conversation
- What am I afraid will happen if I do not defend myself
- How does my defensiveness affect my spouse
- What would listening without responding immediately look like
- How might humility change the tone of our interactions

Part Two

FACING THE DAMAGE

Chapter 4

Accepting Consequences Without Resentment

One of the most challenging parts of genuine change is accepting consequences without resentment.

When awareness turns into ownership and listening replaces defensiveness, a new challenge often emerges. Consequences remain. Trust may not be restored immediately. Relationships may still feel strained. Privileges may be limited. Access may be reduced. This is often where frustration begins to surface.

Many marginal spouses believe that acknowledgment should quickly lead to relief. When it does not, resentment can quietly take root. Resentment says, "I have admitted fault, so why am I still paying the price?"

Scripture offers a different understanding of responsibility.

> *"Do not be deceived, God is not mocked; for whatever a person sows, this he will also reap."*

Galatians 6:7 NASB

Consequences are not punishment. They are the natural outcome of choices and patterns. Accepting them without resentment is a mark of maturity. It reflects an understanding that change is proven over time, not declared in moments.

Resentment often reveals a hidden belief that responsibility should end discomfort. True responsibility accepts discomfort as part of growth.

Accepting consequences means you stop negotiating the cost of change. You stop measuring fairness by how quickly others respond. You remain faithful even when trust is slow to rebuild.

This posture requires humility. It requires patience. It requires surrendering the desire to control outcomes.

BIBLICAL INSIGHT

God Uses Consequences to Refine the Heart

Throughout Scripture, God allows consequences to persist even after repentance. This is not evidence of rejection. It is evidence of refinement.

When David repented, God forgave him. Yet the consequences of his actions are still unfolding. David's growth did not come through avoidance of consequence, but through submission to God within it.

"My sacrifice, O God, is a broken spirit; a broken and a contrite heart You, God, will not despise."

Psalm 51:17 NASB

God does not remove consequences to spare discomfort. He uses them to shape humility, patience, and faithfulness. Consequences become a classroom where character is formed.

Accepting consequences without resentment aligns your heart with God's purposes rather than your preferences.

COUNSELING INSIGHT

Why Resentment Undermines Change

From a counseling perspective, resentment often arises when a person believes they are owed relief for their efforts. This belief turns responsibility into a transaction. "If I admit wrongdoing, things should improve." When improvement is delayed, resentment grows.

Resentment signals that ownership has become conditional.

Conditional responsibility sounds cooperative on the surface, but internally, it resists submission. It measures progress by how others respond rather than by internal change.

Counseling work emphasizes that trust is rebuilt through consistency over time. Consequences protect relationships while trust is being reestablished. They are not barriers to connection. They are safeguards.

When resentment is present, it often appears as impatience, irritability, withdrawal, or subtle pressure on others to move on. These behaviors undermine the very trust you are seeking to rebuild.

Accepting consequences without resentment demonstrates emotional maturity and sincerity. It communicates that change is not performance, but commitment.

COUNSELING APPLICATION

Accepting Consequences with Humility

1. Internal Awareness (Heart Work)
The marginal spouse identifies resentment when consequences persist longer than expected.

2. Behavioral Shift (Observable Action)
The marginal spouse remains faithful without negotiating or demanding relief.

3. Relational Practice (How Others Experience Change)
Others experience sincerity when patience replaces entitlement.

4. Sustainability Check (Accountability and Consistency)
The marginal spouse processes resentment honestly with support rather than acting it out.

GUIDED PRAYER

A Prayer for Humility and Patience

Lord God,

I acknowledge that accepting consequences is difficult for me. I confess that I sometimes expect relief before trust is rebuilt. I ask You to shape my heart so that I can accept responsibility without resentment.

Teach me to remain faithful when outcomes are slow in coming. Please help me release my desire to control timing, responses, and results. Give me patience where I feel frustrated and humility where I feel entitled.

Use this season to refine my character. Help me to trust that You are at work even when progress feels quiet and unseen.

I surrender my expectations to You and commit to walking in obedience regardless of outcome.

In Jesus' name,
Amen.

Reflecting on Consequences

Write honestly and without self-judgment.

• What consequences am I currently resisting
• Where do I feel resentment beginning to surface
• What expectations do I have about how others should respond to my change
• How might patience strengthen my character
• What would faithfulness look like without immediate reward

Chapter 5

Consistency Over Time

Changes that last are rarely dramatic.

It is consistent.

Many marginal spouses attempt to repair damage through intensity. They make strong declarations. They promise change. They show brief bursts of effort. When immediate relief does not follow, discouragement sets in, and old patterns quietly return. This cycle reinforces mistrust and deepens confusion for both spouses.

Consistency is different. Consistency does not rely on emotion or motivation. It is the daily decision to respond differently, even when no one applauds. It is the willingness to show up the same way when things feel calm and when they feel uncomfortable.

Scripture emphasizes the power of steady faithfulness.

> *"Moreover, it is required of stewards that one be found trustworthy."*
>
> **1 Corinthians 4:2 NASB**

Trustworthiness is not built through moments of intensity. It is built through repeated, predictable choices over time. Consistency communicates sincerity. It shows that change is not a performance, but a commitment.

For the marginal partner, consistency often requires resisting the urge to manage outcomes. You may want reassurance that things are improving. You may wish to acknowledge effort. Yet proper consistency continues even when affirmation is limited.

Consistency also exposes patterns. Over time, your responses will either align with your stated desire to change or reveal where resistance still exists. This process requires humility and perseverance.

Becoming whole again means choosing faithfulness over flair and endurance over urgency.

BIBLICAL INSIGHT

Faithfulness in Small Things

Scripture repeatedly highlights the importance of consistency in spiritual growth. God values faithfulness in ordinary obedience more than dramatic declarations.

"One who is faithful in a minimal thing is also faithful in much."

Luke 16:10 NASB

Faithfulness is demonstrated in small, repeated actions. Listening without defensiveness. Keeping commitments. Responding with patience, accepting correction, and maintaining humility even when progress feels slow.

God's work of transformation often unfolds quietly. Seeds are planted long before fruit is visible.

"Let us not lose heart in doing good, for in due time we will reap if we do not grow weary"

Galatians 6:9 NASB

Consistency aligns your life with God's timing rather than your own expectations. It reflects trust in His process rather than reliance on your effort.

COUNSELING INSIGHT

Why Consistency Rebuilds Trust

From a counseling perspective, trust is rebuilt through predictability. When behavior becomes consistent, anxiety decreases. Others no longer have to brace for sudden shifts or reversals. Stability creates emotional safety.

Inconsistency, even when well-intentioned, creates uncertainty in relationships. One good week followed by withdrawal or defensiveness erodes confidence. Trust requires the assurance that change will continue regardless of mood or circumstance.

Counseling work emphasizes that consistency must be observable. Internal resolve is essential, but trust is rebuilt through visible behavior over time. This includes follow-through, emotional availability, and willingness to remain accountable.

Consistency also protects against discouragement. When change is measured by daily faithfulness rather than immediate outcomes, setbacks become learning moments rather than reasons to quit.

COUNSELING APPLICATION

Choosing Faithfulness Over Intensity

1. Internal Awareness (Heart Work)
The marginal spouse experiences urges to change rather than live it consistently.

2. Behavioral Shift (Observable Action)
The marginal spouse practices predictable follow-through rather than dramatic effort.

3. Relational Practice (How Others Experience Change)
Consistency creates safety and reduces anxiety.

4. Sustainability Check (Accountability and Consistency)
The marginal spouse focuses on reliability over time rather than on emotional motivation.

GUIDED PRAYER

A Prayer for Endurance and Faithfulness

Lord God,

I ask You to help me choose faithfulness over intensity. Teach me to remain consistent even when I feel tired, unseen, or discouraged. Strengthen my resolve to live differently day by day.

When I am tempted to make changes rather than commit to them, bring conviction. Where I grow weary of waiting for trust to rebuild, give me patience. Help me trust Your timing and remain obedient regardless of outcome.

Form my character through steady obedience. Make me reliable, teachable, and humble as I walk this path of restoration.

In Jesus' name,
Amen.

Reflecting on Consistency

Take time to reflect honestly.

- In what areas do I tend to rely on intensity instead of consistency
- What behaviors need to become predictable in my life
- How do I respond when change feels unnoticed
- Where am I tempted to give up when progress feels slow
- What would daily faithfulness look like over the next thirty days

Chapter 6

Learning to Repair Without Defensiveness

Repair is one of the most evident signs of genuine change.

It is also one of the most challenging skills to learn.

Repair means acknowledging harm and taking steps to address it without minimizing, justifying, or shifting responsibility. For many marginal spouses, repair feels threatening because it requires vulnerability. It requires admitting that something you did or failed to do caused pain, even if that pain was unintentional.

Defensiveness often reappears during attempts at repair. You may feel misunderstood. You may believe the issue has already been addressed. You may feel tempted to explain your intent or to point out how much effort you are making now. Yet repair that is paired with defensiveness rarely restores trust.

Scripture calls us to a different posture.

> *"Therefore, if you are presenting your offering at the altar, and there you remember that your brother has something against you, leave your offering there before the altar and go; first be reconciled to your brother, and then come and present your offering."*
>
> **Matthew 5:23 24 NASB**

Repair prioritizes reconciliation over self-protection. It centers the experience of the harmed individual rather than the comfort of the person taking responsibility.

Learning to repair without defensiveness requires patience. It means listening again, even when the issue feels repetitive. It means acknowledging the impact without disputing the facts. It means allowing space for pain without trying to manage it.

Repair does not demand perfection. It demands sincerity.

BIBLICAL INSIGHT

God Values Reconciliation and Humility

Throughout Scripture, reconciliation is presented as a sacred responsibility. God consistently values humility over self-justification and restoration over image.

"Be kind to one another, tender-hearted, forgiving each other, just as God in Christ also has forgiven you."

Ephesians 4:32 NASB

Forgiveness does not eliminate the need for repair. It creates an environment in which repair can occur. God models repair through confession, repentance, and restoration.

When Zacchaeus encountered Jesus, his repentance was not verbal alone. He took concrete steps to repair harm.

"If I have defrauded anyone of anything, I will give back four times as much."

Luke 19:8 NASB

Biblical repair involves acknowledgment, responsibility, and action. It reflects a heart that prioritizes restoration over comfort.

COUNSELING INSIGHT

What Repair Actually Requires

From a counseling perspective, repair is not merely an apology. An apology acknowledges wrongdoing. Repair addresses impact and demonstrates change.

Effective repair includes listening to how the other person was affected, validating their experience, and taking steps to prevent the harm from recurring. Defensiveness interrupts this process by shifting focus back to the self.

Many marginal spouses struggle with repair because they equate it with weakness. In reality, repair requires emotional strength. It requires the ability to tolerate discomfort without escaping or controlling the conversation.

Counseling work emphasizes that repeated repair builds trust when it is paired with consistent change. Trust is restored not because mistakes never happen, but because repair happens reliably and sincerely.

COUNSELING APPLICATION

Repairing Without Defensiveness

1. Internal Awareness (Heart Work)
The marginal spouse experiences fear when asked to acknowledge harm.

2. Behavioral Shift (Observable Action)
The marginal spouse acknowledges the impact but does not explain the intent.

3. Relational Practice (How Others Experience Change)
Repair builds trust when the spouse feels heard rather than debated.

4. Sustainability Check (Accountability and Consistency)
The marginal spouse repeatedly practices repair, not selectively.

GUIDED PRAYER

A Prayer for Humility and Repair

Lord God,

I ask you to teach me how to repair without defending myself. Please help me to listen fully and respond with humility when I have caused harm.

Please give me the courage to acknowledge the impact without minimizing or explaining it. Shape my heart to value reconciliation more than comfort and restoration more than image.

Where I am tempted to protect myself, remind me that You are my defender. Teach me to walk in humility and sincerity as I seek to repair what has been damaged.

In Jesus' name,
Amen.

Reflecting on Repair

Write honestly and thoughtfully.

- When do I become defensive during attempts to repair
- What fears arise when I am asked to acknowledge impact
- How do my repair attempts affect my spouse
- What would a sincere repair look like without explanation or justification
- How can I demonstrate repair through consistent action

Part Three

REBUILDING TRUST AND SAFETY

Chapter 7

Understanding Trust as a Process

Trust is not restored by intention.

It is rebuilt through a process.

Many marginal spouses believe that trust should be restored once responsibility is acknowledged and behavior begins to change. When trust does not follow effort immediately, frustration often arises. You may wonder why your spouse remains guarded or hesitant even after you have admitted fault and begun making changes.

Trust does not return because words have changed. It returns because patterns have changed over time.

Trust is formed through consistency, transparency, and reliability. It is fragile after damage and must be handled with patience. Attempting to rush trust often undermines it further. Pressure communicates entitlement rather than humility.

Scripture recognizes trust as something that develops through proven character.

> *"The integrity of the upright will guide them."*

Proverbs 11:3 NASB

Integrity is not proven in moments of clarity. It is demonstrated through repeated alignment between words and actions. Trust grows when your spouse can predict your response, rely on your commitments, and observe change without fear of reversal.

Understanding trust as a process requires releasing control. You do not get to decide when trust is restored. You can determine whether you will remain faithful while it is rebuilt.

BIBLICAL INSIGHT

Faithfulness Precedes Trust

Scripture teaches that trust is connected to faithfulness. God does not entrust responsibility prematurely. He observes obedience over time.

> *"One who is faithful in a minimal thing is also faithful in much."*

Luke 16:10 NASB

Trust follows faithfulness. It is never demanded. It is given when reliability has been demonstrated.

God Himself models this process. Throughout Scripture, God gradually entrusts responsibility as obedience is proven. This pattern is not punishment. It is wisdom.

When you accept trust as a process rather than an entitlement, your posture shifts from impatience to perseverance.

COUNSELING INSIGHT

Why Rushing Trust Backfires

From a counseling perspective, trust is rebuilt when the nervous system feels safe. Following relational harm, the injured spouse often remains attuned to inconsistencies. This is not bitterness. It is self-protection.

Attempts to rush trust often sound like pressure. Statements such as "I have changed" or "How long will this take?" communicate impatience rather than understanding. Even subtle pressure can cause withdrawal.

Counseling work emphasizes that trust is rebuilt through predictability. The injured spouse needs time to observe that the change is stable and not situational. When trust is allowed to return naturally, it is stronger and more sustainable.

Patience is not passive. It is an active commitment without demand.

COUNSELING APPLICATION

Allowing Trust to Rebuild Gradually

1. Internal Awareness (Heart Work)
The marginal spouse recognizes impatience with the process of rebuilding trust.

2. Behavioral Shift (Observable Action)
The marginal spouse continues faithfulness without seeking reassurance.

3. Relational Practice (How Others Experience Change)
Trust grows as predictability replaces pressure.

4. Sustainability Check (Accountability and Consistency)
The marginal spouse resists measuring progress by emotional response.

GUIDED PRAYER

A Prayer for Patience in the Process

Lord God,

I confess that I want trust to return quickly. I struggle with waiting and uncertainty. Help me release control over outcomes and commit to faithfulness instead.

Teach me to be patient without pressure. Help me remain consistent without seeking reassurance. Shape my heart so that I value integrity more than validation.

I place this process in Your hands. Give me endurance to remain obedient even when trust is slow to return.

In Jesus' name,
Amen.

Reflecting on Trust

Take time to reflect honestly.

- How do I respond when trust is not immediately restored
- Where do I feel tempted to pressure or rush the process
- What behaviors demonstrate reliability over time
- How can I remain faithful without expecting reassurance
- What does integrity look like in this season

Chapter 8

Accountability That Leads to Growth

Accountability is often misunderstood.

It is not control. It is care.

Many marginal spouses resist accountability because it feels restrictive or humiliating. It may feel like supervision rather than support. Yet accountability is one of the clearest indicators that change is sincere and ongoing. It provides structure where patterns once went unchecked and clarity where confusion once lived.

Accountability begins when you invite truth into your life rather than managing it from a distance. It means allowing others to observe your behavior, ask questions, and speak honestly without retaliation or withdrawal. This posture requires humility and courage.

Scripture presents accountability as a safeguard rather than a threat.

> *"Two are better than one because they have a good return for their labor. For if either of them falls, the one will lift up his companion."*
>
> **Ecclesiastes 4:9-10 NASB**

Accountability does not exist to shame you. It exists to support growth and prevent regression. It helps interrupt old patterns before they regain strength.

Healthy accountability focuses on responsibility rather than punishment. It encourages honesty. It reinforces consistency. It reminds you that change is sustained through community, not isolation.

BIBLICAL INSIGHT

God Uses Accountability to Protect His People

Throughout Scripture, God places people in accountable relationships. He sends mentors and leaders to confront, guide, and restore. Accountability is one of the means God uses to keep His people aligned with truth.

> "Iron sharpens iron, so one person sharpens another."
>
> **Proverbs 27:17 NASB**

Sharpening is not always comfortable, but it is purposeful. God does not call His people to walk alone. Accountability protects against self-deception and gradual drift.

When accountability is resisted, isolation increases. When accountability is welcomed, growth is strengthened.

COUNSELING INSIGHT

What Healthy Accountability Looks Like

From a counseling perspective, healthy accountability is clear, consistent, and agreed upon. It is not vague or reactive. It includes defined expectations, regular check-ins, and openness to feedback.

Effective accountability partners are not those who merely affirm you. They are those who will tell you the truth without attacking you and support you without enabling old behavior.

Accountability that leads to growth requires your participation. You must be willing to report honestly, receive correction without defensiveness, and follow through on commitments. When accountability is used to manage perception rather than promote change, it loses its power.

Growth occurs when accountability is embraced as a gift rather than endured as a burden.

COUNSELING APPLICATION

Welcoming Accountability

1. Internal Awareness (Heart Work)
The marginal spouse identifies fear associated with oversight or correction.

2. Behavioral Shift (Observable Action)
The marginal spouse agrees to clear accountability expectations.

3. Relational Practice (How Others Experience Change)
Others experience reliability rather than defensiveness.

4. Sustainability Check (Accountability and Consistency)
The marginal spouse maintains accountability even when trust improves.

GUIDED PRAYER

A Prayer for Humility and Support

Lord God,

I acknowledge that I cannot change in isolation. I ask You to give me humility to welcome accountability rather than resist it.

Please help me choose honesty over image and growth over comfort. Please guide me to wise and godly support that will challenge me with truth and walk with me in faithfulness.

Teach me to receive correction without defensiveness and encouragement without pride. Use accountability to strengthen my character and protect me from falling back into old patterns.

In Jesus' name,
Amen.

Reflecting on Accountability

Write honestly and without self-protection.

- What fears do I associate with accountability
- Where have I resisted oversight or feedback
- Who could provide wise and godly accountability in my life
- What expectations or boundaries would support growth
- How can accountability help me remain consistent over time

Chapter 9

Rebuilding Safety Through Transparency

Safety is rebuilt through transparency, not reassurance.

Many marginal spouses attempt to restore a sense of safety by offering words of comfort. They promise honesty. They assure their spouse that things will be different. While reassurance may feel sincere, it rarely rebuilds a sense of safety on its own. Safety is formed when behavior becomes visible, consistent, and predictable over time.

Transparency means allowing your life to be seen without resistance. It involves open communication, transparent decision-making, and a willingness to answer questions without irritation or defensiveness. Transparency removes secrecy and replaces it with credibility.

Scripture calls believers to live openly.

> *"But if we walk in the Light as He Himself is in the Light, we have fellowship with one another"*

1 John 1:7 NASB

Walking in the light requires humility. It requires releasing control over information and accepting responsibility for how choices affect others. Transparency is not about self-exposure for attention. It is about integrity.

For the marginal spouse, transparency may initially feel intrusive. You may feel monitored or questioned. Yet transparency is not surveillance. It is the rebuilding of trust through openness. Safety grows when your spouse no longer has to guess, investigate, or brace for hidden information.

BIBLICAL INSIGHT

God Brings Healing Through the Light

Scripture consistently connects light with truth and restoration. God exposes what is hidden not to shame, but to heal.

> *"For nothing is hidden that will not become evident, nor anything secret that will not be known and come to light."*

Luke 8:17 NASB

What remains hidden often maintains power. What is brought into the light can be addressed, forgiven, and redeemed. Walking openly before God and others reflects trust in grace rather than reliance on concealment.

Transparency aligns your life with God's character. God is faithful, consistent, and truthful. When you walk in the light, you reflect His nature.

COUNSELING INSIGHT

Why Transparency Creates Safety

From a counseling perspective, safety is restored when anxiety decreases. Anxiety decreases when information is reliable, consistent, and freely offered.

Secrecy fuels hypervigilance. Transparency reduces the need for monitoring. When your spouse knows that information will not be withheld or minimized, emotional safety begins to return.

Transparency must be proactive. Waiting to disclose until questioned undermines trust. Offering information freely communicates sincerity and stability.

Transparency is not temporary. It continues long after trust begins to rebuild. When openness becomes a way of life, safety becomes internal rather than conditional.

COUNSELING APPLICATION

Practicing Transparency

1. Internal Awareness (Heart Work)
The marginal spouse notices resistance to openness.

2. Behavioral Shift (Observable Action)
The marginal spouse offers information freely rather than reactively.

3. Relational Practice (How Others Experience Change)
Transparency reduces anxiety and restores safety.

4. Sustainability Check (Accountability and Consistency)
The marginal spouse sustains openness as a lifestyle.

GUIDED PRAYER

A Prayer for Walking in Truth

Lord God,

Help me walk in truth without fear. Where I have hidden, avoided, or controlled information, bring conviction and courage.

Teach me to choose transparency over comfort. Help me trust that walking in the light leads to healing. Please give me the humility to answer honestly and the patience to remain open, even when it feels uncomfortable.

Remove secrecy from my life and replace it with integrity. Let my actions reflect faithfulness, and my words reflect truth.

In Jesus' name,
Amen.

Reflecting on Transparency

- What areas of my life have lacked transparency
- How does secrecy affect safety in my marriage
- Where do I feel most resistant to openness
- What would proactive transparency look like daily
- How can openness demonstrate sincerity over time

Part Four

IDENTITY AND INTERNAL TRANSFORMATION

Chapter 10

Rebuilding Identity Beyond Old Patterns

Lasting change requires more than new behavior.

It requires a renewed identity.

Many marginal spouses attempt to change while holding onto the same internal identity. They try to behave differently while still seeing themselves as justified, misunderstood, or entitled. When identity remains unchanged, old patterns eventually return.

Becoming whole again means allowing God to reshape how you see yourself. Your identity can no longer be rooted in control, avoidance, superiority, or self-protection. It must be grounded in truth, humility, and responsibility.

Scripture speaks clearly about transformation.

> "And do not be conformed to this world, but be transformed by the renewing of your mind"
>
> **Romans 12:2 NASB**

Renewal begins internally. When identity shifts, behavior follows. When identity remains unchanged, behavior becomes performance.

Rebuilding identity requires letting go of old narratives. Narratives that justified distance. Narratives that minimize harm. Narratives that protected pride. God invites you into a new way of seeing yourself and others.

BIBLICAL INSIGHT

Becoming a New Creation

Scripture teaches that identity transformation is central to Christian growth. In Christ, believers are not simply improved; they are transformed. They are renewed.

> *"Therefore, if anyone is in Christ, this person is a new creation; the old things passed away; behold, new things have come."*
>
> **2 Corinthians 5:17 NASB**

A new identity does not erase responsibility. It empowers it. When you see yourself as accountable before God rather than defensive before others, humility grows.

God does not call you to manage appearances. He calls you to walk in truth. Identity rooted in Christ produces consistency, sincerity, and maturity.

COUNSELING INSIGHT

Why Identity Change Sustains Growth

From a counseling perspective, behavior change without identity change is fragile. When stress increases, old identities resurface, and old patterns reemerge.

Identity shapes automatic responses. When your identity shifts from self-protection to responsibility, your reactions change naturally. You no longer respond out of fear or entitlement, but out of integrity.

Counseling work emphasizes that lasting change occurs when individuals internalize new values rather than comply externally. Identity change creates stability by aligning motivation with behavior.

COUNSELING APPLICATION

Reforming Identity

1. Internal Awareness (Heart Work)
The marginal spouse identifies old narratives shaping reactions.

2. Behavioral Shift (Observable Action)
The marginal spouse practices responses aligned with renewed identity.

3. Relational Practice (How Others Experience Change)
Change feels authentic rather than performative.

4. Sustainability Check (Accountability and Consistency)
The marginal spouse reinforces a new identity through daily obedience.

GUIDED PRAYER

A Prayer for Renewed Identity

Lord God,

I ask you to reshape how I see myself. Where my identity has been formed by fear, control, or avoidance, bring renewal.

Teach me to see myself as accountable, humble, and dependent on You. Help me let go of old narratives that no longer align with the truth. Renew my mind and transform my heart.

May my identity be rooted in obedience and integrity rather than self-protection. Lead me as I become whole again.

In Jesus' name,
Amen.

Reflecting on Identity

- What identities have shaped my behavior in the past
- How do these identities affect my reactions
- What new identity is God inviting me to embrace
- Where do I resist letting go of old narratives
- How would a renewed identity change daily choices

Chapter 11

Responding to Setbacks Without Returning to Old Patterns

Setbacks are not evidence that change has failed.

There is evidence that growth continues.

Every process of transformation includes moments of regression, frustration, or discouragement. Old habits may resurface under stress. Emotional reactions may emerge unexpectedly. You may find yourself responding in ways you thought you had left behind. What matters most in these moments is not the setback itself, but how you react to it.

Marginal patterns often reappear when pressure increases. Fatigue, conflict, disappointment, or fear can trigger familiar responses such as withdrawal, defensiveness, control, or avoidance. The temptation is to view setbacks as proof that change is pointless or temporary. This belief often leads to discouragement or resignation.

Scripture offers a steadier perspective.

> *"For a righteous person falls seven times, and rises again."*
>
> **Proverbs 24:16 NASB**

Growth is not linear. The absence of struggle does not prove wholeness, but by the willingness to rise, repent, and re-engage. Setbacks become destructive only when they are used as justification to return permanently to old patterns.

Responding well to setbacks requires honesty. It requires acknowledging the misstep without minimizing it or collapsing into shame. It requires returning to responsibility quickly rather than retreating into avoidance.

Becoming whole again means learning to interrupt old cycles before they regain control.

BIBLICAL INSIGHT

Grace That Leads Forward

Scripture consistently reveals a God who responds to failure with invitation rather than rejection. God does not excuse sin, but He also does not abandon those who return to Him with humility.

> *"My little children, I am writing these things to you so that you may not sin. And if anyone sins, we have an Advocate with the Father, Jesus Christ the righteous."*
>
> **1 John 2:1 NASB**

Grace does not eliminate responsibility. It strengthens it. God's grace creates space for repentance and renewal, not permission to remain unchanged.

Responding to setbacks with humility aligns you with God's character. Returning quickly to the truth demonstrates maturity and sincerity.

COUNSELING INSIGHT

Why Recovery Matters More Than Perfection

From a counseling perspective, recovery after a setback is more important than flawless behavior. Trust is not rebuilt because mistakes never happen. It is rebuilt because mistakes are honestly addressed and consistently repaired.

When a setback occurs, the injured spouse often watches closely. Not to punish, but to see whether change is stable. Quick ownership, repair, and accountability reassure safety. Avoidance or defensiveness reinforces fear.

Counseling emphasizes that setbacks can actually strengthen trust when handled well. They demonstrate that change is not dependent on ideal circumstances, but is rooted in commitment.

Learning to respond differently after a setback is a significant marker of growth.

COUNSELING APPLICATION

Responding Well to Setbacks

1. Internal Awareness (Heart Work)
The marginal spouse recognizes shame or avoidance after missteps.

2. Behavioral Shift (Observable Action)
The marginal spouse returns quickly to responsibility and repair.

3. Relational Practice (How Others Experience Change)
Quick ownership restores confidence.

4. Sustainability Check (Accountability and Consistency)
The marginal spouse treats setbacks as opportunities for growth.

GUIDED PRAYER

A Prayer for Returning to Truth

Lord God,

I acknowledge that setbacks discourage me. I ask you to help me respond with humility rather than shame or avoidance.

When old patterns surface, help me return quickly to truth. Please give me the courage to admit failure, seek forgiveness, and make amends. Strengthening my resolve to continue growing rather than retreating.

Thank you for being so gracious as to invite me forward. Teach me to rise again with honesty and responsibility.

In Jesus' name,
Amen.

Reflecting on Setbacks

- What situations tend to trigger old patterns
- How do I usually respond after a setback
- Where am I tempted to justify or minimize missteps
- What would a healthy recovery look like in real time
- How can setbacks become opportunities for growth

Chapter 12

Replacing Old Coping Strategies with Healthy Responses

Lasting change requires more than stopping harmful behavior.

It requires learning new ways to respond.

Marginal behavior is often supported by coping strategies that once felt necessary. Withdrawal may have reduced conflict. Control may have provided security. Silence may have avoided vulnerability. Over time, these strategies became familiar responses rather than intentional choices.

Becoming whole again means identifying these old coping strategies and intentionally replacing them with healthier responses. This process requires awareness, practice, and patience.

Scripture calls believers to active renewal.

> *"Lay aside the old self, which is being corrupted in accordance with the lusts of deceit, and put on the new self."*
>
> **Ephesians 4:22-24 NASB**

Change is both removal and replacement. Old patterns must be laid aside, and new responses must be practiced until they become natural.

Healthy responses often feel unfamiliar at first. Engagement may feel risky. Transparency may feel exposed. Emotional availability may feel uncomfortable. Yet growth requires moving toward what is healthy rather than retreating into what is familiar.

BIBLICAL INSIGHT

Putting On the New Self

Scripture teaches that transformation involves intentional participation. God provides power for change, but He also calls His people to choose obedience daily.

> *"Therefore, consider the members of your earthly body as dead to immorality, impurity, passion, evil desire, and greed."*
>
> **Colossians 3:5 NASB**

Letting go of old coping strategies requires recognizing their impact and choosing new responses that align with truth and humility. God does not merely call you away from harmful behavior. He calls you toward maturity.

COUNSELING INSIGHT

How New Patterns Are Formed

From a counseling perspective, coping strategies are replaced through repetition. New responses must be practiced consistently, especially under stress. This may include learning to communicate directly, tolerate discomfort, ask for help, or remain present during conflict.

Old strategies will attempt to resurface when stress increases. This does not mean failure. This indicates that the new pattern is still forming. Persistence is key.

Counseling work emphasizes that growth accelerates when new responses are reinforced through accountability, reflection, and prayer. Over time, what once felt difficult becomes more natural.

Replacing coping strategies is not about becoming someone else. It is about becoming whole.

COUNSELING APPLICATION

Replacing Old Coping Strategies

1. Internal Awareness (Heart Work)
The marginal spouse identifies familiar escape behaviors.

2. Behavioral Shift (Observable Action)
The marginal spouse consistently practices healthier responses.

3. Relational Practice (How Others Experience Change)
Presence replaces distance.

4. Sustainability Check (Accountability and Consistency)
New responses are reinforced through repetition and support.

GUIDED PRAYER

A Prayer for New Responses

Lord God,

I ask you to help me release the coping strategies that no longer align with the truth. Where I have relied on avoidance, control, or silence, teach me healthier ways to respond.

Please give me the courage to practice new responses even when they feel uncomfortable. Strengthen me to remain present, honest, and engaged. Shape my habits so that my reactions reflect integrity and maturity.

I submit my growth to You and trust You to lead me into wholeness.

In Jesus' name,
Amen.

Reflecting on Coping Strategies

- What coping strategies have shaped my behavior
- How have these strategies affected my marriage
- Which new responses feel most uncomfortable
- What situations require intentional practice
- How can I support new patterns through accountability

Part Five

LIVING WHOLE AND SUSTAINING CHANGE

Chapter 13

Learning to Lead with Humility

Leadership in marriage is not proven through authority.

It is revealed through humility.

Many marginal spouses confuse leadership with control. They assume leadership means having the final word, setting direction without input, or maintaining influence through distance or intimidation. Biblical leadership is different. It is rooted in service, responsibility, and submission to God.

Jesus redefined leadership by modeling humility.

> *"Whoever wants to become great among you shall be your servant."*
>
> **Matthew 20:26, NASB**

Humility does not diminish leadership. It strengthens it. Humble leadership creates safety. It invites trust. It communicates that power will not be used to dominate or silence.

Learning to lead with humility requires relinquishing entitlement. Leadership in marriage is not claimed by position. It is earned through consistent character. When humility is present, leadership becomes trustworthy rather than threatening.

For the marginal spouse, humility may require acknowledging past misuse of authority. It may require stepping back, listening more, and allowing others to influence decisions. This is not a weakness. It is wisdom.

BIBLICAL INSIGHT

Christlike Leadership

Scripture presents Christ as the model of humble leadership. Though He possessed all authority, He chose service.

> *"Have this attitude in yourselves which was also in Christ Jesus."*
>
> **Philippians 2:5 NASB**

Jesus led through sacrifice, patience, and truth. He did not force obedience. He invited transformation. When leadership reflects Christ's humility, it becomes life-giving rather than controlling.

COUNSELING INSIGHT

Why Humility Restores Trust

From a counseling perspective, humility reduces fear. When a spouse senses that power will not be misused, emotional safety increases. Humility signals that leadership is no longer self-focused, but relationally aware.

Counseling work emphasizes that humility is demonstrated through behavior, not declarations. Listening, collaboration, and accountability communicate humility far more clearly than words ever could.

Leadership grounded in humility creates space for healing rather than resistance.

COUNSELING APPLICATION

Leading with Humility

1. Internal Awareness (Heart Work)
The marginal spouse examines entitlement and control.

2. Behavioral Shift (Observable Action)
Leadership is expressed through service and listening.

3. Relational Practice (How Others Experience Change)
Humility creates trust rather than fear.

4. Sustainability Check (Accountability and Consistency)
Leadership remains accountable and relational.

GUIDED PRAYER

A Prayer for Humble Leadership

Lord God,

Teach me to lead with humility rather than control. Where I have relied on authority rather than service, it has brought conviction and change.

Help me reflect Christ's leadership through patience, integrity, and care. Remove entitlement from my heart and replace it with humility. Shape my leadership to build trust rather than fear.

In Jesus' name,
Amen.

Reflecting on Leadership

- How have I defined leadership in the past
- Where has control replaced humility
- How does humility change the way I lead
- What behaviors communicate safety and trust
- How can leadership reflect Christ more clearly

Chapter 14

Rebuilding Emotional Availability

Emotional availability is not automatic.

It is cultivated.

Many marginal spouses struggle with emotional availability because vulnerability feels unsafe. Emotions may have been ignored, minimized, or managed through distance. Over time, emotional withdrawal becomes familiar and comfortable.

Rebuilding emotional availability requires learning to remain present with feelings rather than escaping them. It involves listening with empathy, responding with care, and engaging emotionally even when it feels uncomfortable.

Scripture affirms emotional presence.

> *"Rejoice with those who rejoice, and weep with those who weep."*

Romans 12:15 NASB

Emotional availability communicates care. It signals that your spouse's inner world matters. Without it, intimacy cannot be sustained.

Becoming whole again requires allowing emotions to be expressed and received without judgment or avoidance.

BIBLICAL INSIGHT

God Is Emotionally Present

Scripture reveals a God who is emotionally engaged with His people. God listens. God responds. God draws near.

> *"The Lord is near to the brokenhearted."*

Psalm 34:18 NASB

Emotional availability reflects God's character. When you learn to remain present emotionally, you reflect His compassion and care.

COUNSELING INSIGHT

Why Emotional Availability Feels Risky

From a counseling perspective, emotional withdrawal often develops as protection. Being emotionally present feels vulnerable. It removes the distance that once provided control or safety.

Counseling work emphasizes that emotional availability is essential for trust and connection. Without it, relationships become functional but distant. Rebuilding availability requires patience and practice.

COUNSELING APPLICATION

Building Emotional Availability

1. Internal Awareness (Heart Work)
The marginal spouse notices discomfort with vulnerability.

2. Behavioral Shift (Observable Action)
The marginal spouse engages emotionally rather than withdrawing.

3. Relational Practice (How Others Experience Change)
Emotional presence increases intimacy.

4. Sustainability Check (Accountability and Consistency)
Availability becomes intentional and practiced.

GUIDED PRAYER

A Prayer for Emotional Presence

Lord God,

Help me remain emotionally present rather than withdrawing. Teach me to listen with empathy and respond with care.

Where fear has kept me distant, bring courage. Where avoidance has shaped my habits, bring change. Help me reflect Your compassion and presence in my relationships.

In Jesus' name,
Amen.

Reflecting on Emotional Availability

- When do I withdraw emotionally
- What emotions feel hardest to engage
- How does emotional availability affect intimacy
- What small steps can increase presence
- How can empathy reshape my responses

Chapter 15

Repairing Trust Through Daily Faithfulness

Trust is rebuilt through daily faithfulness, not grand gestures.

Many marginal spouses attempt to restore trust through dramatic acts or declarations. While these may feel meaningful, trust is rebuilt through consistent, ordinary obedience over time.

Scripture highlights the value of faithfulness.

> *"Moreover, it is required of stewards that one be found trustworthy."*

1 Corinthians 4:2 NASB

Daily faithfulness includes honesty, reliability, follow-through, and emotional presence. These behaviors create predictability. Predictability creates safety. Safety allows trust to return gradually.

Repairing trust requires patience. It requires continuing to show up even when progress feels slow. Faithfulness is proven when no one is watching and when affirmation is limited.

BIBLICAL INSIGHT

God Honors Faithfulness

Throughout Scripture, God honors faithfulness more than performance. Obedience over time reflects trust in God rather than reliance on self-effort.

> *"Let us not lose heart in doing good,"*

Galatians 6:9 NASB

Faithfulness aligns your life with God's purposes and timing.

COUNSELING INSIGHT

How Trust Is Sustained

From a counseling perspective, trust is sustained through consistency. When behavior becomes predictable, anxiety decreases. Trust grows when promises are kept, and actions align with words.

Counseling work emphasizes that trust rebuilding is gradual. It cannot be rushed or demanded. Daily faithfulness creates the foundation for lasting restoration.

COUNSELING APPLICATION

Practicing Daily Faithfulness

1. Internal Awareness (Heart Work)
The marginal spouse resists seeking dramatic validation.

2. Behavioral Shift (Observable Action)
Faithfulness is expressed in ordinary consistency.

3. Relational Practice (How Others Experience Change)
Trust grows through predictability.

4. Sustainability Check (Accountability and Consistency)
The marginal spouse remains steady without recognition.

GUIDED PRAYER

A Prayer for Faithful Living

Lord God,

Please help me choose daily faithfulness over quick results. Strengthen my commitment to live with integrity, consistency, and humility.

Teach me to trust Your timing and remain obedient even when progress feels slow. Shape my character through steady faithfulness.

In Jesus' name,
Amen.

Reflecting on Faithfulness

- What does daily faithfulness look like for me
- Where am I tempted to seek quick results
- How does consistency build trust
- What habits support reliability
- How can faithfulness reflect my growth

Part Six

WALKING FORWARD IN WHOLENESS

Chapter 16

Living Changed Without Managing Outcomes

One of the final tests of genuine change is learning to live differently without managing results.

Many marginal spouses make progress but remain focused on outcomes. They watch for signs of approval. They look for reassurance. They measure success by whether trust is restored quickly or relationships feel easier. When outcomes lag behind effort, discouragement or resentment can quietly return.

Living changed means remaining faithful even when results are uncertain. It means choosing obedience without using it to control responses. Actual change does not depend on how others react. It is anchored in integrity before God.

Scripture calls believers to obedience rather than outcome control.

> *"So then, my beloved, just as you have always obeyed, not as in my presence only, but now much more in my absence, work out your salvation with fear and trembling."*
>
> **Philippians 2:12 NASB**

When you live changed without managing outcomes, your focus shifts from performance to faithfulness. You stop asking whether change is being noticed and start asking whether your life aligns with truth.

This posture frees you from pressure. It allows growth to continue without manipulation or self-protection. It reflects trust in God rather than reliance on validation.

BIBLICAL INSIGHT

Obedience Without Conditions

Scripture consistently teaches that obedience is offered to God, not negotiated with people. Faithfulness is not dependent on reward. It is an act of trust.

> *"Commit your works to the Lord, and your plans will be established."*
>
> **Proverbs 16:3 NASB**

God does not promise immediate results. He promises His presence and guidance. When obedience is offered without conditions, it becomes an act of worship rather than a strategy.

Living changed without managing outcomes aligns your heart with God's sovereignty.

COUNSELING INSIGHT

Why Outcome Control Undermines Growth

From a counseling perspective, outcome control keeps change externally focused. When desired responses drive behavior, it becomes conditional. Conditional change is fragile.

Outcome control often shows up as subtle pressure, emotional withdrawal, or discouragement when validation is absent. These behaviors can quietly undermine trust.

Counseling work emphasizes that sustainable change is internally motivated. When growth is rooted in values and identity rather than reward, it remains stable even under stress.

COUNSELING APPLICATION

Releasing Outcome Control

1. Internal Awareness (Heart Work)
The marginal spouse notices a desire to manage responses.

2. Behavioral Shift (Observable Action)
Obedience continues regardless of feedback.

3. Relational Practice (How Others Experience Change)
Change feels sincere rather than strategic.

4. Sustainability Check (Accountability and Consistency)
Faithfulness remains internally motivated.

GUIDED PRAYER

A Prayer for Faithfulness Without Control

Lord God,

I release my need to manage outcomes. Teach me to live changed, not because it guarantees results, but because it honors You.

Help me trust Your timing and remain faithful even when progress feels unseen. Remove the desire to control responses and replace it with obedience and peace.

I place my growth in Your hands and commit to walking in integrity regardless of outcome.

In Jesus' name,
Amen.

Reflecting on Outcomes

- Where do I feel tempted to manage results
- How do unmet expectations affect my behavior
- What would faithfulness look like without validation
- How can I trust God with outcomes
- What internal values guide my change

Chapter 17

When Change Is Tested Over Time

Time reveals the truth of transformation.

Change is often easiest in the beginning. Motivation is high. Awareness is fresh. Commitment feels strong. Over time, however, novelty fades and routine returns. This is where change is tested.

Long-term change requires endurance. It requires maintaining integrity when attention fades, and effort feels ordinary. Many marginal spouses struggle here. They mistake endurance for stagnation or assume that difficulty means failure.

Scripture reminds us that perseverance is essential.

"Blessed is a man who perseveres under trial."

James 1:12 NASB

Change that endures is demonstrated over time. It is proven through consistency on ordinary days, in difficult seasons, and in quiet moments when no one is watching.

When change is tested, old patterns may attempt to resurface. Fatigue, stress, or disappointment can trigger familiar responses. What matters is not the presence of temptation, but the reaction to it.

BIBLICAL INSIGHT

Endurance Produces Maturity

Scripture consistently links endurance with spiritual maturity.

"And let endurance have its perfect result, so that you may be perfect and complete, lacking in nothing."

James 1:4 NASB.

God uses time to deepen character. He uses endurance to refine motives and strengthen faith. When change is sustained over time, it becomes part of who you are rather than something you are trying to do.

COUNSELING INSIGHT

Why Long-Term Change Requires Structure

From a counseling perspective, long-term change requires intentional support. Motivation alone is not enough. Structure helps maintain consistency when enthusiasm fades.

The structure may include routines, accountability, reflection, and ongoing learning. Without structure, stress often pulls individuals back into familiar patterns.

Counseling work emphasizes that realistic expectations support endurance. Growth is not constant improvement. It includes plateaus, challenges, and renewed commitment.

COUNSELING APPLICATION

Enduring Over Time

1. Internal Awareness (Heart Work)
The marginal spouse recognizes fatigue or discouragement.

2. Behavioral Shift (Observable Action)
Commitment continues through structure and routine.

3. Relational Practice (How Others Experience Change)
Stability replaces unpredictability.

4. Sustainability Check (Accountability and Consistency)
Endurance is supported through continued accountability.

GUIDED PRAYER

A Prayer for Endurance

Lord God,

Strengthen me to remain faithful over time. When change feels ordinary or complex, help me persevere.

Protect me from complacency and discouragement. Give me endurance to continue walking in truth long after motivation fades.

Shape my character through time and teach me to trust Your refining work.

In Jesus' name,
Amen.

Reflecting on Endurance

- What challenges test my commitment to change
- How do I respond when growth feels slow
- What structures support long-term faithfulness
- Where do I need renewed perseverance
- How can endurance deepen my character

Chapter 18

Walking in Integrity Regardless of Response

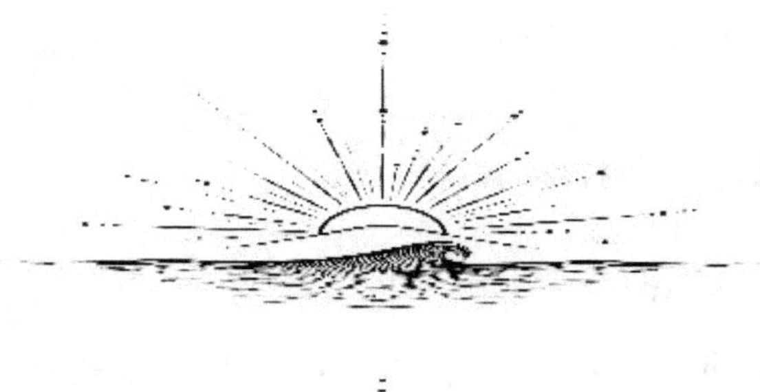

Integrity is revealed when faithfulness continues without recognition.

Walking in integrity means aligning your actions with truth, regardless of how others respond. It means choosing honesty, humility, and consistency even when appreciation is limited or trust remains guarded.

For the marginal partner, this stage represents true maturity. Change is no longer driven by fear, pressure, or outcome. It is rooted in identity and conviction.

Scripture defines integrity clearly.

"The integrity of the upright will guide them."

Proverbs 11:3 NASB

Integrity provides direction when feedback is unclear. It anchors behavior when emotions fluctuate. It allows you to live in peace even when reconciliation is incomplete.

Walking in integrity does not guarantee the restoration of relationships. It ensures alignment with God.

BIBLICAL INSIGHT

God Honors Integrity

Scripture affirms that God values integrity above appearance.

"He who walks in integrity walks securely."

Proverbs 10:9 NASB

Security comes not from approval, but from obedience. Integrity frees you from the need to manage perception, allowing you to live honestly before God and others.

COUNSELING INSIGHT

Integrity as the Foundation of Wholeness

From a counseling perspective, integrity represents internal coherence. Your values, actions, and identity align. This alignment reduces anxiety and increases emotional stability.

When integrity guides behavior, reactions become measured rather than reactive. Decisions reflect principles rather than pressure. This is the essence of wholeness.

Integrity does not depend on others changing. It depends on your commitment to truth.

COUNSELING APPLICATION

Walking in Integrity Regardless of Response

1. Internal Awareness (Heart Work)
The marginal spouse no longer needs approval.

2. Behavioral Shift (Observable Action)
Integrity guides decisions consistently.

3. Relational Practice (How Others Experience Change)
Others experience reliability without pressure.

4. Sustainability Check (Accountability and Consistency)
Integrity is maintained independent of outcome.

GUIDED PRAYER

A Prayer for Integrity

Lord God,

I ask You to anchor my life in integrity. Help me live faithfully regardless of response or recognition.

Remove the need for approval and replace it with conviction. Teach me to walk securely in truth and obedience.

May my life reflect wholeness that honors You and brings peace.

In Jesus' name,
Amen.

Reflecting on Integrity

- How would you now define integrity in your relationship with God, yourself, and your spouse?
- What helps you choose integrity when no one is affirming your growth?
- What does integrity require of you when your spouse is not present, not responsive, or not aware of your effort?
- Where does integrity need to be strengthened through daily obedience?
- How does integrity guide your actions when you no longer try to manage outcomes or responses?

CONCLUSION

Becoming Whole Is a Lifelong Journey

Wholeness is not a destination you arrive at once.

It is a way of living you choose daily.

Throughout this book, you have been invited to move beyond awareness to ownership, beyond intention to consistency, and beyond performance to integrity. You have been asked to examine patterns, accept responsibility, listen without defending, repair without resentment, and walk faithfully even when outcomes remain uncertain.

This journey is not easy. It requires humility. It requires endurance. It requires the courage to remain present when retreat would feel safer. Yet wholeness is worth the cost.

Becoming whole again does not mean you will never struggle. It means you will no longer allow struggle to justify harmful patterns. It means you will respond differently when old impulses surface. It means your identity is no longer shaped by avoidance, control, or fear, but by truth and responsibility before God.

Scripture reminds us that God's work in us is ongoing.

> *"For I am confident of this very thing, that He who began a good work in you will perfect it until the day of Christ Jesus."*

Philippians 1:6 NASB

God does not abandon the work He begins. He shapes it patiently over time. Growth often happens quietly. Change deepens through obedience rather than intensity. Wholeness is revealed through faithfulness when no one is watching.

You may not see immediate restoration in every relationship. Trust may still be rebuilding. Consequences may remain. Responses may be slow or cautious. Yet your responsibility is not to manage results. Your responsibility is to walk in integrity.

Wholeness is not about controlling the future.

It is about honoring God in the present.

As you move forward, remember that actual change is sustained through humility, accountability, and continued dependence on God. Stay teachable. Stay honest. Stay anchored in truth.

This is not the end of the journey.

It is the beginning of a new way of living.

A CALL TO RENEWAL

CHOOSING WHOLENESS DAILY

Renewal is not a single moment of decision.

It is a daily choice.

God invites you to renewal, not as punishment, but as restoration. Renewal begins when you offer yourself honestly to Him, without excuses, conditions, or demands. It continues as you choose obedience even when it is inconvenient or unseen.

> *"Therefore I urge you, brothers and sisters, by the mercies of God, to present your bodies as a living and holy sacrifice, acceptable to God, which is your spiritual service of worship"*
>
> **Romans 12:1 NASB**

To present yourself as a living sacrifice means repeatedly choosing to surrender. It means allowing God to shape your heart, your habits, and your relationships over time. Renewal is sustained through consistency, prayer, and accountability.

As you continue this journey, commit yourself to these practices:

Remain honest when it would be easier to withdraw.
Remain accountable when independence feels safer.

Remain faithful when results are delayed.
Remain humble when pride seeks control.

Renewal does not promise comfort. It promises transformation.

God is not asking you to become someone else.

He is inviting you to become whole.

If you are willing to continue walking in truth, God will continue His work in you. Wholeness is not perfection. It is alignment. It is living with integrity, responsibility, and faithfulness before God and others.

Choose renewal today.

Choose wholeness again tomorrow.

And trust God to lead you forward.

GUIDED PRAYER

A PRAYER OF RENEWAL AND COMMITMENT

Lord God,

I offer myself to You again. I acknowledge that becoming whole is an ongoing journey, and I commit to walking it with humility and truth.

Renew my heart where old patterns try to return. Strengthen my resolve when growth feels slow. Anchor my identity in You rather than in outcomes or approval.

Help me live with integrity, responsibility, and faithfulness. Teach me to trust Your timing and submit to Your work in my life.

I choose renewal today and commit to choosing it again tomorrow.

In Jesus' name,
Amen.

CONTEXTUAL REFLECTION SHEET 1

PRIDE AND AWARENESS

Seeing What God Is Revealing

Book Three begins with awareness. Pride often resists this stage by dulling conviction or reframing responsibility.

As a marginal spouse, reflect honestly.

What patterns described in the early chapters of this book have become harder for me to ignore

Where have I noticed myself becoming defensive as awareness increases?

What explanations have I used to soften or redirect responsibility?

How might pride be shaping the way I interpret my spouse's pain or concerns

Prayerfully ask God to continue revealing truth rather than allowing comfort.

CONTEXTUAL REFLECTION SHEET 2

FROM AWARENESS TO OWNERSHIP

Where Pride Resists Responsibility

This book argues that awareness alone is insufficient. Ownership requires humility.

Where have I acknowledged issues without fully owning my part?

What responsibilities have I delayed, minimized, or expected others to release too quickly?

How has pride influenced my expectations for relief, reassurance, or restored trust

What would full ownership look like without explanation or comparison?

CONTEXTUAL REFLECTION SHEET 3

LISTENING WITHOUT DEFENDING

Humility in Conversation

Listening without defending is a repeated theme in this book because defensiveness blocks healing.

During recent conversations, where did I feel most tempted to defend myself

What fear was driving that defensiveness?

How might humility change the way I listen to my spouse's experience?

What does remaining present without correcting communicate to my spouse?

CONTEXTUAL REFLECTION SHEET 4

CONSEQUENCES AND HEART POSTURE

Responding Without Resentment

Book Three emphasizes that consequences are not punishment but part of growth.

What consequences am I currently experiencing as a result of my past patterns?

How have I responded internally to these consequences?

Where has pride shown up as resentment, entitlement, or impatience?

How does humility reframe consequences as part of God's refining work?

CONTEXTUAL REFLECTION SHEET 5

CONSISTENCY OVER TIME

When Change Feels Ordinary

This book teaches that consistency, not intensity, rebuilds trust.

Where am I tempted to rely on short bursts of effort rather than steady obedience?

How should I respond when change goes unnoticed or is not affirmed?

What does humility require of me on ordinary days when progress feels slow?

How can I measure growth in terms of faithfulness rather than response?

CONTEXTUAL REFLECTION SHEET 6

HUMILITY AND TRUST AS A PROCESS

Trust is presented in this book as a process rather than an entitlement.

Where do I feel most impatient with the pace of trust rebuilding?

How might pride pressure outcomes rather than submit to timing?

What behaviors demonstrate humility while trust is still forming?

How does remaining faithful without reassurance reflect growth?

CONTEXTUAL REFLECTION SHEET 7

IDENTITY AND WHOLENESS

Letting Go of Old Narratives

Becoming whole again requires an identity transformation, not merely behavioral change.

What old narratives about myself have shaped my responses?

How have these narratives supported pride, control, or avoidance?

What new identity is God forming through humility and obedience?

How would living from this renewed identity affect my daily choices?

CONTEXTUAL REFLECTION SHEET 8

LIVING CHANGED WITHOUT MANAGING OUTCOMES

One of the final themes of this book is relinquishing control over outcomes.

Where do I still measure my change by how others respond?

How does pride seek validation or recognition for effort?

What does humility look like when outcomes remain uncertain?

How can I continue living in a changed way that honors God rather than guarantees results?

FINAL INTEGRATION REFLECTION

CHOOSING WHOLENESS DAILY

As you move forward, reflect on the journey this book has guided you through.

What has God revealed to me about pride through this book?

What practices will help me remain humble and accountable?

What does choosing wholeness look like in this season of my life?

Who will support me as I continue walking in truth and responsibility?

CLOSING PRAYER

A Prayer for Humility and Wholeness

Lord God,

Thank you for revealing the truth and inviting me to change.

Where pride has protected my comfort, replace it with humility.

Help me remain present, accountable, and faithful as You continue Your work in me.

Teach me to walk in wholeness, not by controlling outcomes, but by trusting You daily.

In Jesus' name,
Amen.

PRAYERS APPENDIX

BECOMING WHOLE AGAIN

Healing and Responsibility for the Marginal Partner

These prayers are designed for daily reflection, counseling homework, or group use. They may be prayed repeatedly as God continues His work of renewal and transformation.

PRAYER FOR CHAPTER 1

When Awareness Begins

Lord God,

I invite you to search my heart and reveal what I have ignored, minimized, or justified. Please give me the courage to see myself truthfully without fear or defensiveness. Where I have been unaware of my patterns, bring clarity. Where I have resisted conviction, bring humility.

Help me remain open to Your truth and willing to examine my ways. I trust that Your light leads to healing rather than condemnation.

Amen.

PRAYER FOR CHAPTER 2

From Awareness to Ownership

Father,

I acknowledge that awareness alone is not enough. Teach me to take responsibility for my actions without excuses or deflection. Where I have explained rather than owned, it brings conviction. Where I have resisted accountability, bring humility.

Help me walk honestly before You and others. Shape my heart so that ownership becomes a pathway to freedom and growth.

Amen.

PRAYER FOR CHAPTER 3

Listening Without Defending

Lord,

Quiet my need to defend myself. Teach me to listen thoroughly and patiently, even when the truth is uncomfortable. Help me receive others' experiences without interruption, correction, or explanation.

Give me humility to hear before speaking and wisdom to respond with gentleness. Let my listening reflect Your patience and grace.

Amen.

PRAYER FOR CHAPTER 4

Accepting Consequences Without Resentment

God,

I confess that I struggle to accept consequences without frustration. Help me release resentment and trust that You are at work even when outcomes are difficult. Teach me patience and humility as I face the results of my choices.

Use this season to refine my character and strengthen my obedience. I place my expectations in Your hands.

Amen.

PRAYER FOR CHAPTER 5

Consistency Over Time

Lord,

Please help me choose faithfulness over intensity. Teach me to walk consistently even when motivation fades or affirmation is limited. Strengthen my resolve to remain obedient day by day.

Form my character through steady commitment. Make me trustworthy and reliable as I continue growing in wholeness.

Amen.

PRAYER FOR CHAPTER 6

Learning to Repair Without Defensiveness

Father,

Please give me the courage to repair what has been damaged without defending myself. Help me acknowledge impact honestly and take responsibility with humility.

Teach me to value reconciliation over comfort and restoration over image. Let my actions reflect sincerity and care.

Amen.

PRAYER FOR CHAPTER 7

Understanding Trust as a Process

God,

Help me let go of control over the pace of trust rebuilding. Teach me patience and perseverance as I remain faithful without pressure or entitlement.

Strengthen my commitment to integrity and consistency. Help me trust Your timing and remain obedient throughout the process.

Amen.

PRAYER FOR CHAPTER 8

Accountability That Leads to Growth

Lord,

I ask for humility to welcome accountability as a gift rather than a burden. Please guide me to wise support that will speak truth and encourage growth.

Help me remain teachable, honest, and consistent. Use accountability to protect me and strengthen my character.

Amen.

PRAYER FOR CHAPTER 9

Rebuilding Safety Through Transparency

Father,

Teach me to walk in the light with honesty and courage. Remove any desire to hide, control, or withhold truth. Please help me choose transparency even when it feels uncomfortable.

Let my openness rebuild safety and reflect Your integrity. Shape my life so that secrecy no longer has a place.

Amen.

PRAYER FOR CHAPTER 10

Rebuilding Identity Beyond Old Patterns

God,

Renew my mind and reshape my identity. Help me release old narratives that no longer align with the truth. Teach me to see myself as accountable, humble, and dependent on You.

Form my identity around integrity and obedience rather than self-protection or control.

Amen.

PRAYER FOR CHAPTER 11

Responding to Setbacks Without Returning to Old Patterns

Lord,

When setbacks occur, help me respond with humility rather than shame or avoidance. Teach me to return quickly to truth and responsibility.

Strengthen my perseverance and remind me that growth is ongoing. Help me rise again with sincerity and commitment.

Amen.

PRAYER FOR CHAPTER 12

Replacing Old Coping Strategies with Healthy Responses

Father,

Reveal the coping strategies that no longer serve your purposes. Help me lay aside old patterns and practice healthier responses.

Please give me the courage to remain present, honest, and engaged even when it feels unfamiliar. Lead me into wholeness step by step.

Amen.

PRAYER FOR CHAPTER 13

Learning to Lead with Humility

God,

Teach me to lead with humility rather than control. Remove entitlement from my heart and replace it with service and care.

Help my leadership reflect the character of Christ. Let it build trust and create safety in my relationships.

Amen.

PRAYER FOR CHAPTER 14

Rebuilding Emotional Availability

Lord,

Help me remain emotionally present and responsive. Where I have withdrawn or avoided vulnerability, please give me the courage to engage.

Teach me empathy and compassion. Let my presence reflect Your nearness and care.

Amen.

PRAYER FOR CHAPTER 15

Repairing Trust Through Daily Faithfulness

Father,

Strengthen me to live each day faithfully. Help me value consistency over recognition and obedience over immediate results.

Use daily faithfulness to rebuild trust and deepen my character. Teach me patience as You continue Your work.

Amen.

PRAYER FOR CHAPTER 16

Living Changed Without Managing Outcomes

God,

I release my desire to control outcomes. Teach me to live changed because it honors You, not because it guarantees results.

Help me trust Your timing and remain faithful regardless of response. Anchor my life in integrity and peace.

Amen.

PRAYER FOR CHAPTER 17

When Change Is Tested Over Time

Lord,

When change feels difficult or ordinary, give me endurance. Help me remain committed even when progress feels slow.

Use time to refine my character and deepen my faith. Teach me to persevere with humility and hope.

Amen.

PRAYER FOR CHAPTER 18

Walking in Integrity Regardless of Response

Father,

Anchor my life in integrity. Help me live faithfully regardless of recognition or approval.

Remove the need for validation and replace it with conviction. Let my life reflect wholeness, truth, and obedience.

Amen.

Committing to Wholeness

Take time to write prayerfully and honestly.

- What has God revealed to me through this journey
- What patterns am I committed to leaving behind
- What practices will help sustain growth
- Who will support me in accountability
- What does choosing wholeness look like moving forward

Becoming Whole in Practice Worksheets

Guided Worksheets for Responsibility, Humility, and Change

Chapters 1–3

Purpose

This worksheet helps the marginal spouse identify patterns that have shaped distance, harm, or instability in the marriage.

Identifying Patterns

Which marginal patterns described in this book apply to me?

(Check all that apply).

Emotional withdrawal
Defensiveness
Inconsistency
Avoidance of responsibility
Control through silence or distance
Minimizing impact
Spiritualizing without accountability

HOW HAVE THESE PATTERNS SHOWN UP IN MY MARRIAGE

Awareness Without Excuses

When these patterns are named, my usual reaction is

What explanations have I relied on to soften responsibility

What truth feels most uncomfortable to face right now

Prayerful Awareness

Ask God for clarity rather than comfort.

WORKSHEET 2

OWNERSHIP AND RESPONSIBILITY

Chapters 2–4

Purpose

This worksheet moves the marginal spouse from awareness into ownership.

My Responsibility

What behaviors am I responsible for changing?

How have these behaviors affected my spouse emotionally?

Impact Over Intent

What did I intend?

What did my spouse experience?

What responsibility is required of me now?

Ownership Statement

Write one clear ownership statement without explanation.

WORKSHEET 3

LISTENING WITHOUT DEFENDING

Chapter 3

Purpose

This worksheet strengthens humility in communication.

Defensive Triggers

I feel most defensive when

What fear is activated in those moments?

Practicing Humble Listening

During conversations, I will practice

Listening without interrupting

Remaining silent when I want to explain

Acknowledging impact before responding

What makes this difficult for me?

Reflection

How does listening without defending communication change?

WORKSHEET 4

ACCEPTING CONSEQUENCES WITHOUT RESENTMENT

Chapters 4–5

Purpose

This worksheet addresses entitlement and resentment.

Current Consequences

What consequences am I currently facing?

Heart Check

What emotions surface most often?

Which pride-based thoughts arise? (Circle all that apply)

This should be over by now.
I have already admitted this.
I am trying harder than they see.

Humility Reframe

How might God be using these consequences to refine me?

What faithfulness requires of me now?

WORKSHEET 5

CONSISTENCY OVER TIME

Chapters 5–7

Purpose

This worksheet reinforces daily faithfulness.

Patterns of Inconsistency

Where do I tend to start strong but fade?

Daily Commitments

Three behaviors I must practice consistently

Measuring Growth

How will I measure faithfulness without relying on affirmation?

WORKSHEET 6

TRUST AS A PROCESS

Chapters 7–9

Purpose

This worksheet reframes trust rebuilding.

My Expectations

What expectations do I have about trust returning?

Releasing Control

Where do I feel tempted to rush or pressure?

What humility looks like while trust is rebuilding?

Integrity Practice

What predictable behaviors create safety?

WORKSHEET 7

IDENTITY AND INTERNAL CHANGE

Chapters 10–12

Purpose

This worksheet supports identity transformation rather than surface behavior change.

Old Narratives

What beliefs about myself have shaped my responses?

New Identity

Who is God calling me to become through obedience?

Practicing the New Self

What responses reflect my renewed identity?

WORKSHEET 8

RESPONDING TO SETBACKS

Chapter 11

Purpose

This worksheet helps prevent regression into old patterns.

Triggers

What situations tend to pull me back into old responses?

Recovery Plan

When a setback occurs, I will (Circle all that apply)

Acknowledge it quickly
Repair without defensiveness
Return to accountability

Reflection

How can setbacks strengthen trust when handled well?

WORKSHEET 9

LIVING CHANGES WITHOUT MANAGING OUTCOMES

Chapters 16–18

Purpose

This worksheet anchors integrity beyond response or reward.

Outcome Control

Where do I still seek validation or reassurance?

Faithfulness Statement

Even if outcomes do not change, I commit to (*Please finish this statement*)

Integrity Check

How does living change honor, God, regardless of response?

FINAL WORKSHEET

COMMITMENT TO WHOLENESS

Integration *(Answer these questions honestly)*

What this book has revealed about me

What patterns am I leaving behind

What practices will sustain change

Who will support me in accountability

My commitment before God

CLOSING PRAYER

Lord God,

Thank you for leading me through truth, responsibility, and humility.

Help me remain faithful as You continue Your work in me.

I choose wholeness not to manage outcomes, but to honor You with integrity.

In Jesus' name,

Amen.

SCRIPTURE INDEX

Becoming Whole Again
Healing and Responsibility for the Marginal Partner

ECCLESIASTES

4:9–10

The value of support and accountability in growth and restoration.

EPHESIANS

4:22–24

Putting aside old patterns and intentionally putting on a renewed way of living.

4:32

Kindness, compassion, and forgiveness are markers of maturity and healing.

GALATIANS

6:7

The reality of sowing and reaping and accepting consequences without resentment.

6:9

Perseverance in doing good and remaining faithful over time.

HEBREWS

4:12

God's Word reveals thoughts, motives, and areas needing transformation.

JAMES

1:4

Endurance producing maturity and completeness.

1:12

Blessing is promised to those who persevere under trial.

LUKE

16:10

Faithfulness in small things is the foundation for greater trust.

19:8

True repentance is demonstrated through concrete acts of repair.

MATTHEW

5:23–24

The priority of reconciliation and repair before worship.

20:26

Leadership defined through humility and service.

PHILIPPIANS

1:6

Confidence that God continues and completes His work of transformation.

2:5

Adopting the mindset of Christ in humility and obedience.

2:12

Living out obedience without relying on external affirmation.

PROVERBS

10:9

Security is found in walking with integrity.

11:2

Wisdom flows from humility rather than pride.

11:3

Integrity as a guide in rebuilding trust.

16:3

Committing actions to the Lord rather than managing outcomes.

18:13

The danger of speaking before listening.

24:16

Rising again after setbacks as a mark of righteousness.

27:17

Accountability sharpens character and growth.

PSALMS

34:18

God's nearness to the brokenhearted.

51:10

The prayer for inner renewal and a steadfast spirit.

51:17

God's acceptance of humility and contrition.

139:23–24

Inviting God to search the heart and reveal harmful ways.

ROMANS

12:1

Offering oneself as a living sacrifice in ongoing renewal.

12:2

Transformation through the renewing of the mind.

14:12

Personal accountability before God.

1 CORINTHIANS

4:2

Trustworthiness as a requirement of stewardship.

1 JOHN

1:7

Walking in the light as the foundation for fellowship and safety.

2:1

Christ as advocate when failure occurs.

2 CORINTHIANS

5:17

New identity and transformation in Christ.

7:10

Godly sorrow leads to repentance without regret.

2 SAMUEL

12:13

David models ownership and repentance.

JOB

42:5

Transformation through humility and deeper understanding.

~

LAMENTATIONS

3:40

Self-examination leading to repentance and return to the Lord.

~

GENESIS

3:9

God's invitation to awareness and honesty.

WEEKLY SCRIPTURE MEMORY PLAN

Becoming Whole Again

Healing and Responsibility for the Marginal Partner

How to Use This Plan

- Focus on **one verse per week**
- Read the verse **aloud once daily**
- Reflect briefly on how it applies to your behavior and responses
- Use the verse in prayer throughout the week
- Memorization is encouraged, not forced

Progress is measured by **consistency**, not perfection.

WEEK 1

When Awareness Begins

Memory Verse

> *"Search me, O God, and know my heart; and try me and know my anxious thoughts."*

Psalm 139:23 NASB

Weekly Focus

Inviting God into honest self-examination.

WEEK 2

From Awareness to Ownership

Memory Verse

> *"So then each one of us will give an account of himself to God."*

Romans 14:12 NASB

Weekly Focus

Accepting personal responsibility without excuses.

WEEK 3

Listening Without Defending

Memory Verse

> *"One who gives an answer before he hears, it is foolishness and shame to him."*

Proverbs 18:13 NASB

Weekly Focus

Practicing humility and restraint in conversation.

WEEK 4

Accepting Consequences Without Resentment

Memory Verse

> *"Do not be deceived, God is not mocked; for whatever a person sows, this he will also reap."*

Galatians 6:7 NASB

Weekly Focus

Responding to consequences with humility rather than bitterness.

WEEK 5

Consistency Over Time

Memory Verse

> *"Moreover, it is required of stewards that one be found trustworthy."*

1 Corinthians 4:2 NASB

Weekly Focus

Choosing faithfulness over intensity.

WEEK 6

Learning to Repair Without Defensiveness

Memory Verse

"First be reconciled to your brother."

Matthew 5:24 NASB

Weekly Focus

Prioritizing repair and reconciliation.

WEEK 7

Understanding Trust as a Process

Memory Verse

"The integrity of the upright will guide them."

Proverbs 11:3 NASB

Weekly Focus

Allowing trust to rebuild through integrity.

WEEK 8

Accountability That Leads to Growth

Memory Verse

"Iron sharpens iron, so one person sharpens another."

Proverbs 27:17 NASB

Weekly Focus

Welcoming accountability as protection.

WEEK 9

Rebuilding Safety Through Transparency

Memory Verse

"If we walk in the Light as He Himself is in the Light,
we have fellowship with one another."

1 John 1:7 NASB

Weekly Focus

Choosing openness over secrecy.

WEEK 10

Rebuilding Identity Beyond Old Patterns

Memory Verse

> *"Do not be conformed to this world, but be transformed by the renewing of your mind."*

Romans 12:2 NASB

Weekly Focus

Allowing God to reshape identity.

WEEK 11

Responding to Setbacks Without Returning to Old Patterns

Memory Verse

> *"For a righteous person falls seven times, and rises again."*

Proverbs 24:16 NASB

Weekly Focus

Persevering without shame.

WEEK 12

Replacing Old Coping Strategies with Healthy Responses

Memory Verse

> "Lay aside the old self... and put on the new self."

Ephesians 4:22–24 NASB

Weekly Focus

Practicing new, healthier responses.

WEEK 13

Learning to Lead with Humility

Memory Verse

> *"Whoever wants to become great among you shall be your servant."*

Matthew 20:26 NASB

Weekly Focus

Leading through service rather than control.

WEEK 14

Rebuilding Emotional Availability

Memory Verse

> *"Rejoice with those who rejoice, and weep with those who weep."*

Romans 12:15 NASB

Weekly Focus

Practicing empathy and presence.

WEEK 15

Repairing Trust Through Daily Faithfulness

Memory Verse

> *"Let us not lose heart in doing good, for in due time we will reap if we do not grow weary."*

Galatians 6:9 NASB

Weekly Focus

Remaining faithful when progress feels slow.

WEEK 16

Living Changed Without Managing Outcomes

Memory Verse

> *"Commit your works to the Lord, and your plans will be established."*

Proverbs 16:3 NASB

Weekly Focus

Releasing control and trusting God with results.

WEEK 17

When Change Is Tested Over Time

Memory Verse

> *"And let endurance have its perfect result."*

James 1:4 NASB

Weekly Focus

Allowing endurance to shape maturity.

WEEK 18

WALKING IN INTEGRITY REGARDLESS OF RESPONSE

Memory Verse

"He who walks in integrity walks securely."

Proverbs 10:9 NASB

Weekly Focus

Living faithfully without seeking approval.

A WORD OF ENCOURAGEMENT

If you are reading this book, it means you have chosen courage over avoidance.

Growth is rarely comfortable. Becoming whole requires honesty, humility, and perseverance, especially when change exposes areas you would rather leave untouched. If this journey feels slow, heavy, or unsettling at times, that does not mean you are failing. It often indicates that you are confronting the truth rather than avoiding it.

You may be tempted to measure progress by how others respond, how quickly circumstances change, or how often you feel confident. But transformation is not measured by speed or approval. It is measured by faithfulness.

God does not ask you to be perfect.

He asks you to be willing.

There will be days when insight is clear and days when old patterns resurface. Do not let those moments convince you that change is not happening. Growth is proven not by the absence of struggle, but by your willingness to return to truth, take responsibility, and keep walking forward.

Remember this.

Conviction is not condemnation.

Discomfort is not defeat.

Endurance is evidence of growth.

God sees the work you are doing, even when it feels unseen. He honors quiet, consistent, and sincere obedience. When progress feels slow, trust that roots are growing beneath the surface.

> *"The Lord will accomplish what concerns me; Your faithfulness, Lord, is everlasting."*

Psalm 138:8 NASB

Stay present. Stay honest. Stay committed.

You are not walking this path alone, and the work God is doing in you is not wasted. Wholeness is not achieved in a single moment, but it is built one faithful step at a time.

Keep going.

Continue the Journey
Series Closing

THE MARGINAL SPOUSE SERIES

The Marginal Spouse Series is a biblically grounded, counseling-informed collection designed to expose, confront, and heal patterns of marginal behavior within marriage.

Each volume addresses a different dimension of relational dysfunction, responsibility, repentance, and restoration, while centering the reader on truth, clarity, and spiritual strength.

CURRENT & UPCOMING TITLES IN THE SERIES:

• Book One — The Marginal Spouse: Recognizing Destructive Patterns and Restoring Clarity
Introduces the concept of marginal behavior in marriage and helps readers identify unhealthy relational dynamics.

• Book Two — Living with a Marginal Spouse: Faith, Boundaries, and Endurance for the faithful spouse.
Equips responsible spouses with discernment, boundaries, and emotional stability as they navigate brutal marital realities.

• Book Three — Becoming Whole Again: Healing and Responsibility for the Marginal Spouse

Guiding Marginal spouses toward repentance and transformation

• Book Four — Restoring the Marginal Marriage: Rebuilding Trust, Intimacy, and Forgiveness
Explores repentance, accountability, rebuilding trust, and what genuine transformation looks like over time.

• Book Five — Breaking Generational Cycles of Neglect and Dysfunction: Breaking Generational Cycles of Neglect and Dysfunction
Addresses family-of-origin issues, generational dysfunction, and how to interrupt unhealthy cycles for future generations.

• Book Six — Walking Forward in Wisdom: Guarding What Has Been Restored
Guides readers toward long-term emotional health, godly decision-making, and sustainable relational maturity.

Each book can be read independently, but together they provide a comprehensive path toward clarity, healing, and renewal.

CONTACT

For speaking requests, questions, or to share your story, you may contact the author at: Lifechange1@comcast.net

BIBLIOGRAPHY

The Heart of Man and Mental Disorders, Rich Thompson, Biblical Counseling Ministries, Inc., 2012. Second Edition

Solving Marital Problems, Jay E. Adams, Zondervan Publishing, 1983

Marriage and Family, Dr. Nicolas Ellen, Dare2Dream Books, 2009

Suggested Reading:

Love the greatest Thing in the World, *Lewis A. Drummond*

Decision Making & the Will of God, Gary *Frieson*

God's Solution to Life's Problems, Wayne *Mack*

The Word from the Wise, *Henry Brandt*

Discerning Idols(Having a God-*Empowered* Heart), *K.B. Haught*

Happy Even After, *Dr. Nicolas Ellen*

Hearts and Habits, *Greg E. Gifford*

Whiter than Snow, *Paul Tripp*

www.ingramcontent.com/pod-product-compliance
Lightning Source LLC
LaVergne TN
LVHW020715110826
845149LV00012B/2269

* 9 7 9 8 9 9 4 1 9 0 5 4 8 *